FLIP
YOUR
THINKING

MELISSA,

KEEP FLIPPING!

ROB

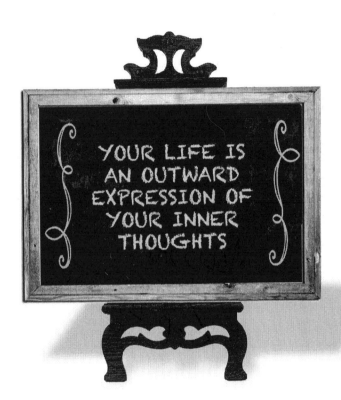

FLIP
YOUR
THINKING
TO IGNITE YOUR WORLD

By Rob Cross

MY GIFT TO YOU

FREE BOOK

As thanks, I offer you
my acclaimed book
SIZZLE SECRETS.
I think you'll love it! It's
packed with useful, timeless
keys to "Keeping Love's Sizzle
When You Keep Love Simple."

GET YOUR FREE COPY HERE
RobFlips.com/special2021

DEDICATION

With a twinkle in my eye and boundless love in my heart, I dedicate this book to my children. And to my children's children. And to their children. As life evolves and we zoom into unchartered futures, it's a safe bet that these same rudimentary truths will still be with us.

ACKNOWLEDGMENTS

Franca, you have been the proof in my puddin'. Your cheers and edifying support-in-action for me through the challenges of this project have confirmed for me the power of love. I would not be the man I am today without you and without that critical third strand, our loving God. We three make a great team, and I am deeply humbled to be your partner.

Oh and, Franca, thank you for saying yes years ago. This author certainly married up!

Table of Contents

HI FRIEND!

*"...Those who cannot change their minds
cannot change anything."*
— George Bernard Shaw

Could it be? Could it possibly be that you and I have been pushing away the very things we desire, all from how we think about them? That has been my experience most of my life. Until I began seeing the irony in life; so much of it seemingly upside-down. My choice to forgive you sets *me* free, not you. Love stays when I let it leave and leaves when I make it stay. My setbacks were only setups for something better. To be heard I needed to talk less.

I challenge you to flip your thinking with every part of your life, from success to marriage. That flipped perspective will introduce you to a whole new ball game of exciting possibilities. Hope abounds, my friend.

My life has been like a big Easter Egg hunt. But the Easter Egg was in my coat pocket all along! And I am thrilled to finally find that egg!

You will discover how your circumstances today are but an outward display of your inward thoughts and beliefs. And the key to having that life you desire starts with flipping how you think.

Author Wayne Dyer understood this. "When you change the way you look at things, the things you look at will change."

I pray my words offer you a new perspective, shifting how you engage with things and people. That will in turn set the stage for fresh, exciting new results. Buckle up, my friend, and let's do some flippin'! I'm truly glad you're here.

Rob

PART ONE

FLIP WHAT YOU MAKE THINGS MEAN

1

FIND YOUR POWER!

THE STORY WE TELL OURSELVES

By the time I showed up on the scene, things were already established and in their places. So, I have limited influence on my life!

FLIP IT Things are whatever <u>you</u> have defined them to be. Nothing present in your life has meaning that was not assigned and/or approved by you.

*"Change how you look at things
and the things you look at will change."*
— Wayne Dyer.

GODISNOWHERE

What did you just read? "God is now here?" Or did you read, "God is nowhere?" Which one is wrong, and which one is right? All that matters is, what you see is what you see. And that's your reality.

You and I both see the same world and the same events. But what meanings you attach to people, things, and occurrences are pivotal. Those meanings are dictating your opinions and choices. If money means "hard to come by," then your financial status will typically prove you right; money will likely show up as a scarce commodity.

The ant looked up at the grape, startled by its enormity. That was just before the elephant passed by and unknowingly stepped on them both. We each see the same grape in life, each from our unique perspective.

 How you think about things is the single biggest influencer of your reality. Your thinking is the very seed of your life experiences.

Seeing relationships as being strenuous will keep you repetitively attracting and creating chaotic relationships. Love doesn't come easy to those who believe relationships are hard.

If you see this world as evil, and the people in it as untrustworthy, then, by golly, you will likely attract and create experiences to confirm your beliefs.

Have you ever tried going right, but you felt pulled to the left? You wanted to lose weight, but you kept eating candy bars and fast foods. You wanted more than anything to have a healthy relationship or make the big bucks or get into shape, and yet you kept falling

Reminder

Your life and everything in it are outward evidence of your inward beliefs.

into the trap of those old self-subverting thoughts and habits.

Eventually you'll give up and stop trying, because you know what the results will be. But wait! Don't quit. Let's try something new! Let's go back to your original, sabotaging belief and...let's FLIP IT!

How you think about things and people will dictate how you respond to and engage with them. If you don't like what's showing up in your life, it might be time to flip your perspective. Otherwise, your life will keep looking like a Friday night rerun.

I once owned a home at the end of my street. One day I walked next door to greet the new neighbors moving in. Their response to my greeting wasn't what I expected. They seemed guarded and unresponsive. I walked back home shaking my head, thinking, "What snobs!"

From that point forward I limited my interactions with them. After all, who wants snobs for neighbors?

A couple of years passed before I was forced to work with them on a street project. While working alongside them, I had a revelation. They were not snobs at all! They were shy.

We became friends, and I still think about the two years of friendship I missed because of my misinterpretation. Plain and simple, I judged them. I held their actions up against my expectation. And they clearly didn't do it my way! They didn't say the right thing and show the right smile at the right moment. They didn't give me what I expected! What's wrong with those people!

But of course, that gaffe wasn't about them at all, was it? It was about my expectations of them. And as we will discuss later, my expectations were merely premeditated resentments.

**Whatever you make things
mean will prescribe how
you interact with them.**

We each established our own perspective on life, way back when we were little ones. We did much of our stamping back then. Crying is bad, stamp! Studying is boring, stamp! Vulnerability is risky, stamp! Showing emotion is weak, stamp!

If you are unsure about what you stamped back then, take a look around you today. Look at your circumstances. Look at your living conditions, your choice of career, the friendships you keep, and the level of chaos in your daily routine. It all reflects your perspective on life.

**Your environment is tangible
evidence of your intangible thoughts.**

Fear of intimacy may show up as having a very limited number of close friends. Fear of failure may have prompted you to create a life of safety. If you play it safe, then you won't have to encounter failure.

Here's What I Figure

Your mind is so powerful that it not only shapes your perception of things, it convinces you that it's the truth. That becomes your reality. Your blind spot is your belief that it was not you who chose what's present in your life now. You believe it was chosen for you. Or maybe the cards were not stacked in your favor.

You alone have determined what you make things mean. If money is scarce and your marriage is hard, those conditions are direct outcomes of your beliefs.

The question of who's right or wrong is a moot question. Whatever is

Reminder

Your Judgments Constrict your world, your Curiosity Expands it

"right" in your mind materializes into your experience of life. I personally believe that self-employment means freedom rather than risk, and so freedom shows up in my face every day. God gave you and me the freedom to choose what we will make things mean. What a gift! Thank you, God!

Mark 11:24 says, "I tell you, whatever you ask for in prayer, believe that you have received it, and it will be yours."

That's powerful! Did you read that? Whatever you believe strongly, it's yours! Of course, there's a caveat: you can't fake a belief. You don't "try hard" to believe something. Your beliefs are fixed, as fixed as the rising sun and the blooming cotton.

Your beliefs are etched on your soul's notepad as they show up in real life. Fortunately, you and I can change a disempowering belief.

Margaret was a single working parent living in Houston. She loathed her motherly role. "It's just so hard being a single mom! And my kids are so unappreciative!" I watched this play out through time as she drudged through her days. Is being a single mom dreadful? Or was that simply her perspective?

Shifting how you see things and people, and redefining what they mean to you, will profoundly change your interactions with them, which in turn changes your experiences with them. And the icing on the cake: more times than not your new perspective will change them in some way!

Change how you feel about single-parenting, and you will completely alter your parenting experience. Determine in your mind that it's a blessing many others are denied. Countless infertile women would give their right arm to have your "parenting issues."

Flipping your perspective will have you waking up a bit lighter. You'll engage with your kids differently. Your newfound take on parenting will even alter your children's demeanor, which in turn will give you an entirely different parental experience.

Reminder

Know your Limits
then ignore them

Kendall was a hardworking executive assistant living in a New York high-rise. At age twenty-nine she had given up on men. They were all jerks! Every one of them. So, I ask you: are all men jerks? Gosh, I hope not. But in her world and in her experiences, all the men she had encountered were worthless. And sadly, her beliefs will continue proving her right as she continues attracting jerks.

I read an article recently entitled, "Why You Must Never Get Married." The author had one too many disappointing experiences with marriage, and so she deemed it something to avoid. And she was doing the world a favor by warning us all to steer clear.

 What we think about things influences how we interact with them, which determines how they unfold in our everyday lives.

That woman viewed marriage as a horrible experience and so she will choose to either avoid marriage or she will create another horrible experience. Or...who knows, she may pick up a copy of my book and decide to FLIP IT!

A flipped perspective would allow her to see her own experiences as a chance to learn and grow and to own her part. And from there she would create something different in her future. Isn't that what life is truly about?

You and I are always either in a state of resisting or receiving the lesson. I want you to always be open for the receiving. Otherwise, you'll get sent back to repeat the class!

How do you see strangers? Do you think of them as potential friends, or do you see them as off-limit? And, what about that homeless guy that you are currently parked next to at the world's longest stoplight? As you sit there awkwardly avoiding eye contact with him, do you view him as someone to avoid? Or do you look past that unbathed surface and recognize his pain? He has a story, just like everyone else. Do you consider that he's like you, except for the few bad choices that landed him there?

Do you view your world through eyes of judgment or curiosity?

My friend, your life is limitless! You can be who and what you want to be. You can accomplish whatever you choose in your mind to accomplish because you were created with abundance in mind. You were crafted from love on purpose. You have it all! Perhaps you've covered up your brilliance with a few layers of doubt and dismay. But we will be shaking those off in short order.

Do You Have Legs? Wow, What a Privilege!

Imagine having no arms or legs. Imagine not being able to walk or even care for your basic needs.

Imagine for a moment not having the ability to wrap your arms around your loved ones. What kind of living hell would that be? Meet Nicholas Vujicic. Nick was born in 1982 in Melbourne, Australia. He had no arms and no legs at birth.

The early days were a struggle for Nick. Beyond the typical adolescent challenges at school, Nick struggled with depression and loneliness. He was constantly faced with the question of "why." Why was he so different than the other kids? He questioned his purpose in life, or if he even had a purpose.

How Nick chose to think about things and what they mean determined what he eventually became. He could have justifiably called himself a victim. He could have made his affliction mean "limited" or even helpless. He certainly could have seen life as a big poker game where he lost. Who could blame him?

Nick made a different choice. He made a gutsy choice. He flipped his perspective on life.

Since his first speaking engagement at age nineteen, he has traveled around the world to share his story with millions. Today, Nick has accomplished more than most people achieve in a lifetime. He's an author, musician, and actor. He enjoys fishing, painting, and swimming.

His choices have led him to a full, productive, and fulfilling life. He's even married now with children! It's all because of what he made his disability mean and not mean.

This man is my inspiration, and frankly, my hero. Beyond most anyone I've known, he is "walking" proof that you can change things by changing the way you think about them. Do yourself a favor; read more about Nick Vujicic.

I am truly thrilled that you are here. I'm not here to motivate you or cheer you on. I'm here to deliver a message that can dramatically alter your course forever. I will be challenging you to FLIP IT. Flip the way you think and feel about everything in your world.

BOTTOM LINE ⌣

It's time to assign new meanings. Garner the power of your thoughts. Real and lasting change starts by flipping your thinking before engaging your feet! If not, you'll simply keep running in circles.

I challenge you to approach this book as if you really don't know everything you think you know. Be open and curious. Be willing to question how you've been looking at things and how you've defined things. If you don't like what you see in life, you picked a bad view. Let's stand up and change the view. Gaining a new perspective can literally save your life. Happy Flipping

2

IT'S YOU,
IT'S ALWAYS BEEN YOU

THE STORY WE TELL OURSELVES

I was born on the wrong side of the tracks. My surroundings have molded me into who I am today.

FLIP IT You are not a product of your environment. Your environment is a product of you. And your circumstances are only mirroring your internal beliefs.

*"Your world mirrors
your thoughts."
— Rob*

My dad religiously punched the clock at Hughes Tool Company, where he was faithfully employed for forty years. Back then many men in the Houston area worked for Hughes, a company that played a major role in the oil industry.

I admired my father for his attitude. No matter how hard that man worked, he never said "no" to throwing a baseball in the backyard. I can see him now, walking in the back door with those worn boots and dusty jeans, but always with a spark in his eye! Thanks, Dad.

My mom ran the household and kept us children fed, watered, and loved. Every recollection of my childhood seems to include Mom. We felt safe and loved in that simple barefoot-cozy life.

From my humble beginnings, I unknowingly set a mental ceiling on my financial future. I started my first business at twenty-one, but my thoughts never allowed me to dream too loftily. Why? I figured that's just not who I am.

I once heard a story about twin brothers who were born in South Texas. This story gave my thinking a major flip.

The two boys were raised by their drunken, aloof father. When it came time to leave the household, they each went their separate way. One boy had actually made something of himself and became a respected professional. But his twin followed the path of their father.

When the destitute brother was asked what made his life take such a turn, he answered, "With a dad like that, how could I possibly become anything different?" When the successful professional was asked what inspired him to such levels of achievement, he answered, "With a dad like that, how could I possibly become anything different?" Each boy chose his own meaning, thereby paving his own path.

I got the message! I possess the power to assign meaning to things. And growing up in a lower-middle-class family didn't mean I had to stay there! To be sure, your past does not equal your present, unless you make it so.

Here's What I Figure

A caged animal becomes a product of his environment. But you and I have the power of choice.

If you claim to be a product of your environment, then you've surrendered your life's helm. You've let your surroundings influence you, rather than you yourself being the influencer.

Whenever you resign your thinking to this notion that you are merely a product of "out there," then you have to invent a story to keep your sanity. And your story becomes your excuse.

Here's a story I told myself for many years: No one in my family is or ever was a writer of any sort. And so why would I even think that I could write a book? It's not in my DNA. Heck, I even hated English class back in the day, so case closed! Any questions?

So, I had my story. And my story kept me safe from having to put my butt on the line.

Was my self-assessment correct? Was I wrong? Everybody has an opinion. And of course, at that time in my life, the only opinion that mattered was my own. So, my belief became my truth, which showed up as my reality. And my reality looked very "average" and unaccomplished.

Reminder

Have the guts to own your part in creating your environment ♥

You might think, "Really? Can my thoughts really be that powerful?"

Yes, they can. And yes, they are. Everything in your environment, from your financial status to your quality of social life, began with your thoughts. You "thought" them into existence.

But wait! I have some great news for you. Little did I know that my past failures were honing me and conditioning me for my present and future success. Yes!

It's not your environment that has been making you into your adorable self. It's your *response* to your environment that's been doing all that fine-tuning. You are consistently given the choice to become a crusty failure or a seasoned warrior.

 I used to pray for God to make my environment better, but God was using my environment to make me better. Hello!

Your seemingly unsupportive environment will either swallow you up or stiffen your resolve to become better. Don't take the bait! Refuse to be bitter. But remember, with that choice to become better comes responsibilities. The day that you decide to own it is the day you must enroll in the school of life. Sound that school bell, baby, it's time to learn!

Your world is like a big mirror, my friend. Your finances, your friends, your activities, your home atmosphere, and even the temperament of your dog; they are all a mirror of yourself. And they are here for you to take notice and learn.

Your futile attempts to change the world around you are only keeping you from true and lasting growth. And it's that growth that will bring you the gold!

> **Reminder**
> Be the change you want to see in the world. *Gandhi*

Do you want friendlier friends? Then be more friendly. Do you want more love? Then practice being more loving.

If you don't like how someone treats you, then pay attention. No, not to them, silly; to yourself! Rather than simply dismissing them as a jerk, ask the hard questions. Ask yourself how you might have been prompting that response. What are you assuming, what are you expecting, what are you inciting? Have the guts to say no to the easy route of blaming and judging.

IT'S A SETUP!

In what ways are you setting yourself up for what you're receiving in your life?

Now, don't run off with this idea like a dog that just stole a rib from the smokehouse! I'm not suggesting that you take the blame or the fault. Instead, I am challenging you to take ownership of your choices. That's a far different animal than blaming or fault-finding.

Rich was my favorite running buddy before he passed away with cancer. He lived life in full color! One day he received a nasty email from his ex-girlfriend. She held back nothing in her rant. I remember asking him how he felt about the letter. In his usual slow, methodical response he told me, "Well, I want to take whatever value it may have for me. There must be some useful takeaway."

Rich taught me much and I carry his spirit with me. Miss you, Rich.

JOHNNY AND THE OYSTERS

Johnny's job was to shell six bushels of oysters for the restaurant's grand opening. That's over 700 oysters! He didn't miss a beat, attacking the chore with a smile and a whistle. When asked how he could possibly be so happy with such a daunting task, he replied, "Heck, with this many shells, there must be a pearl in here somewhere!

BOTTOM LINE ⌣

If you want to change your world, then start by changing you. If you want to change your spouse, then change you. If you want to change your children, then change you. If you want to change your income or your status or your dirty socks, then change you. (I threw that last one in there to make sure you're paying attention.)

How do you change you? When you pay attention to life's hints and nudges from people and things, you'll begin to notice messages being delivered to you on a silver platter.

Not to worry for now. You and I are about to go on a journey of "the new you." And you are going to love the new you!

You are here on this great planet for more than just working, eating, shopping, watching baseball, and raising rug rats. There's another level to life that is waiting for you, my friend. This life isn't so much about becoming someone you're not as it is about a journey back to yourself.

When you look outside yourself at your circumstances, you're looking into a mirror. The environment you attracted reflects your judgments and beliefs about yourself. From your choice of friends to your choice of career, they all reveal who you are and what you think about yourself.

That self-reveal is valuable information that you will either use to further you or reject to restrict and inhibit you.

3

LIFE HAPPENS
<u>FOR</u> YOU,
NOT TO YOU

THE STORY WE TELL OURSELVES

It's not fair! Bad things keep happening to good people! I don't deserve that!

FLIP IT **Things keep happening FOR you, not TO you.**

> *"Everything that happens does so at the right moment and in the right way. You don't have to like it, but it sure makes life smoother when you accept it."*
> *— Rob*

What if everything bad going on around you is only doing you a big favor?

Here's the good news: Nothing "bad" ever happens to you in life. I hear you; it looks bad, smells bad, and so it must be bad. But I assure you, those "bad" experiences are trying to set you up for something good. All you have to do is pay attention.

My filmmaking business was in its eighth consecutive year of high profits and top awards. I had built a strong profile of five-star reviews and accolades. Looking forward in time, I saw nothing but clear skies and a rosy forecast. Until...

That dreaded ninth year arrived. That's when the bottom dropped out without warning. It was like someone pulled a lever and my bookings took a sudden nosedive. I was stunned. How could this possibly be? It made no sense to me. Shaking it off, I was certain the law of averages would bring it all back. It always does.

Not only did bookings not come back, but the following year was even worse! Associates kept asking me the same predictable question: "What happened?" I had no answer for them. Nothing had changed. Nothing had shifted. All my advertising was still in place. I was as passionate as always. And to top it off, the economy was better than it had ever been! It simply made no sense. My thriving business came to a screeching halt and there was no explanation for it.

So, what was my answer? What will I make of it? In my earlier days, panic would have been my M.O. I would have kicked into "victim gear" while frantically finding every conceivable explanation to justify and explain away what was happening to me. And any efforts to create more income would have been from a position of hysteria.

We humans love to have answers, don't we? It gives us a sense of control and feeling on top of it all. But I had no answer for this one. I was baffled with the "what happened?" question. And then I remembered. I reminded myself of what I had been learning and sharing through recent years:

LIFE DOESN'T HAPPEN TO YOU, IT HAPPENS FOR YOU.

Ah-hah! All I needed was a little shift of my perspective! I had been trying to figure out what life was doing to me. Now it was time to stop and listen. Listen to life. Listen to the voice of God.

When I flipped my thinking and began seeing it all from a different angle, my world changed. Everything changed. As I got curious, I began asking the juicy questions: What was life trying to create on my behalf? Where was it wanting to take me? What was it teaching me? What message was written on the wall that I was missing? When I stopped judging and got curious, the barn doors opened!

Reminder

Life's not out to Getcha, it's out to Enricha!

That shift in perspective not only helped keep me sane but also helped clear my vision. It enabled me to maneuver through what would normally feel like a calamity. My decision to Flip my thinking introduced me to a new life. I was stuck and didn't even know it! My tunnel vision was keeping me from what I now clearly see: my purpose.

HERE'S WHAT I FIGURE

Whenever life becomes all about avoiding problems, I tend to take my "eye off the ball." My blinders keep me living in a bubble and ignoring the real issue at hand.

Life is a roller-coaster ride, not a merry-go-round. All those ups and downs and fast turns are here for good reasons. They're not here to scare or defeat you, but rather to stir, excite, ignite, and guide you. Life is vibrant and full of adventure! Whoa, that thought just gave me goosebumps!

I no longer pray that God will grant me a smooth path, but to grant me the strength, discernment, and wisdom to succeed. I no longer seek to be protected. I seek to be equipped.

I LOVE MY COZY!

Comfort zones are the best. They're just so darn safe and free from risks and ruckus and crocodiles and uncomfortable moments and those bad guys. Let me tell you about my comfort zone. It's a doozy! I have it furnished with Blue Bell ice cream and kettle-fried potato chips. How about yours? Oh, and did I mention that your comfort zone will keep you miles and miles away from your purpose and your life potential? Oh yeah, that.

We are not designed to camp in our comfort zone. That zone is a rest stop for you to catch your breath and maybe go potty. God has big plans waiting for you beyond that comfort zone.

Remember that every emotion or upset, and every challenge or "bad news," carries with them a gift. What you might think of as bad or undesirable is simply "it is what it is." It's here FOR you. But there's a caveat: You must be willing to recognize the gift and actively receive it.

Reminder

Go Within or
you'll Go Without

That sudden drop in my business didn't happen *to* me but happened *for* me. And if not for that business loss, I may have never yanked my head out of the sand long enough to consider something bigger in life. Because of that business loss, I'm now exactly where I'm supposed to be. I transitioned from a money-focused career to a purpose-driven adventure.

And get this: I still get to make money to boot! How about them apples!

What about you? Have the years somewhat lulled you into a life of reruns? Are you in touch with your unique purpose in life?

God taps us on the shoulder. I believe He speaks through various people and events. And, now and then, those God-taps have to be upgraded to nudges.

Sometimes those nudges graduate to a shove. And then there's the super-upgrade special that has my name on it. It looks like a two-by-four. I hate that two-by-four! But it's here to serve us.

Bottom Line

I want you to flip how you think about adversity. The victim-thinking will keep you holding back and skirting obstacles. See adversity and setbacks as healthy pruning. Take whatever issue is in front of you, grab it by the horns, and FLIP IT! Get hungry to know what you are being taught. Stay open with curiosity rather than closed with judgment. Know that whatever you are up against is here on your behalf.

Maybe you're being nudged to change direction or to get better at what you're doing. Perhaps this is a boot camp preparation for your upcoming leap from minor to major league. God may have already prepared the way and cleared your path that you are unable to see from your current clouded view.

Do more discerning and less dismissing. Try making sense of what may look like a setback. What is it telling you about yourself? Take your focus off the market swing or your boss's bad haircut or your partner's ugly words. Take your focus off everything outside of yourself and just get still. Look within or you'll go without.

Never slam the gavel down to dismiss your circumstances as being "bad." See them as a necessary piece to a perfect puzzle. You don't have to understand it all right now. You only have to accept it. Otherwise, you'll keep fighting it.

As you flip your thinking with this, you'll see an entirely different view of your predicament. You'll find real answers, rather than escape routes or quick fixes. You'll find expansion, rather than contraction. You'll experience growth instead of repeated lessons. And you'll graduate instead of being sent back to summer school. Yes!

And there's a bonus when you flip your thinking. You'll find new opportunities, ideas, and creative solutions that you would have never found back when you were fighting, avoiding, dismissing, and blaming.

Every event, movie, emotion, book, sermon, market crash, spoiled plans, dashed hopes, and disappointments are here on your behalf. They each hold value. So, look for the blessings and the lessons. And remember, some blessings are cleverly disguised. So, be alert. This world needs more "lerts."

4

SETBACKS ARE
SETUPS WEARING
FUNNY HATS

THE STORY WE TELL OURSELVES

Setbacks are killing me! Just when I start making headway, I get knocked back again!

FLIP IT   **What looks like a setback is only setting you UP for something bigger, better, and far juicier!**

"Take heart. Even when you're stumbling, at least you're stumbling forward."
— Rob

Your setback is like the lock 'n load of a gun, setting you up for something special.

I watched as my friend Sandy struggled to raise her teenage daughter. I was a single parent myself, so I'm familiar with the tremendous attention and love a teenage girl needs to help her gracefully move through those teen years.

Her daughter was a human wrecking ball. I watched that girl generate one calamity after another, from totaling her car to attempted suicide. Were those episodes setbacks? They certainly felt so at the time. Frankly, I wondered if anything good would ever come of her life.

Fast forward fifteen years. She is now responsibly employed. And more gratifying, she is helping other girls cope with their own teen struggles. Today she profoundly impacts the lives of other girls, all because of her earlier debacles.

Who would have thought, way back then, that her destructive years would someday serve the world?

You and I are each writing our story, and setbacks are necessary chapters in that story. Your setback may be trying to teach you, hone you, or maybe even to redirect you.

All those setbacks I experienced through the years were certainly not on my schedule, and they were a thorn in my side as I tried staying on course and sticking with my plans.

I couldn't bring myself to accept the tragic and heart-wrenching loss of my big brother Chris at an early age. And I scratched and clawed as I watched my business crash and burn.

I felt my energy and vitality drop as I clinched in resistance to what I saw as past setbacks. And if someone asked me during those moments how I was doing, I lied like a rug and answered, "Just fine, thanks." I wasn't just fine. And as I kept that resistive tunnel vision with it all, I was unknowingly sitting out the dance.

I'm dancing now, baby! I get it! Yeehaw!

In hindsight, I see how my business crash was necessary. Without that loss, I wouldn't be serving and writing and speaking and coaching and dancing and living out my purpose as I'm doing now.

At times it's necessary for one door to close so  another door can open.

Life's a setup! God was setting me up for something much bigger! And so, in hindsight, my setback was only a course correction.

Here's What I Figure

Once again, I think of life's metaphors. Consider contrasts. Look around you and notice how shades are distinguished from brightness. Sunrays laser through the clouds. Crashing waves break the still waters. A mountain is a mountain, only because there's a valley. Almost everything you see is what it is because of its contrast.

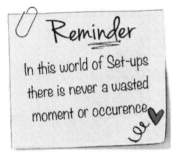

Reminder

In this world of Set-ups there is never a wasted moment or occurence

Can you imagine everything being gray and flat and tasteless? Didn't our Maker do a bang-up job giving us contrasts, colors, and flavors? And when was the last time you threw back your head toward the sky and hollered, "Thank you! You did well!"

Come sit right here with me, I want to remind you of something important: your setback is a contrast that's merely setting you up! Whether you see it or not, it's there.

A black fly on a black wall has no definition. There's purpose behind every event you and I call a setback. In my world, every setback gives me the invitation to step back and redefine myself. I get to ditch a few bad habits and misconceptions, and I'm challenged to re-tweak my faith. It helps me sharpen and refine my values, skills, and my very reason for being here.

It gives me pause for the flaws! It awakens me and shakes my timbers!

Bottom Line

I want you to give that next failure or loss or spoiled plan a big FLIP. Flip your thinking! Whatever meaning you choose to attach to it is what will expand for you. So, choose well. Determine what it is that you really want to expand in your life.

Call it a failure? Then a failure it will be. But when you proclaim, "This is a setup for something bigger," you've positioned yourself to stay open and engaging. You'll then be poised for the learning. In that mind-set, your curiosity is keen, and your senses are heightened while your resources are on full alert. You are primed and ready!

Reminder

Don't allow your fear of setbacks to steal your opportunities for Set-ups

Do you think a professional basketball player stomps away pouting after missing a shot? They're like a sponge, taking in information. That missed shot was a learning opportunity. They're assessing what they did and how they can do it better the next time. They are 100 percent committed to not wasting that shot, but rather to using it.

When you are up against a setback, challenge, or loss, take a deep breath. Remember that your strongest muscle, your mind, is about to assign meaning to that event or circumstance. But *this* time put a big checkmark next to "setup." Acknowledge that you cannot possibly see where this is taking you, but you can choose to believe that it's taking you somewhere better. Ask God to guide your path, to honor your attitude, and to bless your good intentions.

Life is that staircase that you cannot see. The room is dark, but you take the first step anyway, knowing that the rest of the staircase will appear as you need it. This is what faith looks like.

When I divorced, I insisted on knowing why and how. I refused to let it be a setback. I went through those initial days of anger and upset, but as I regained perspective, I was ready for class. I was determined that this would never happen again. And if I had to draw a line through my life history of where my accelerated growth began, the line would be drawn smack dab through the middle of that very day. Imagine that, my life took an exciting turn the day I suffered that setback, all because of my choice to flip what I made it all mean.

Always know that any stumble is a stumble forward. See your setback as a necessary piece to the puzzle. It holds value for you, so take its value, get better, and most importantly, keep moving forward.

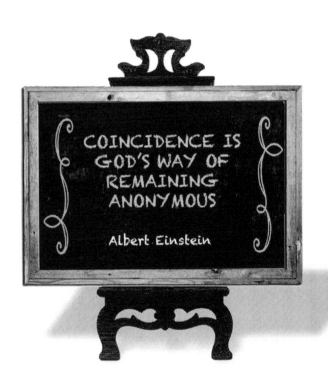

5

COINCIDENCE?
THINK AGAIN

THE STORY WE TELL OURSELVES

Things happen randomly. Now and then it may seem miraculous, but it's all just coincidence.

FLIP IT **Was it a coincidence? Or was it Divine Alignment?**

"Coincidence is a word some jaybird made up who couldn't explain the miracle."
— Rob

Your world around you is acting out a play of intentional design, even when it looks quite arbitrary.

Every person, every event, every thought, or emotion that crosses your path did so for a reason. "Coincidences" and "accidents" are happening all around you, constantly buzzing right past you. Zzzoom! There went one right there, did you see it?

Your role is to recognize those "coincidences" and to pluck from them what gift they have for you in the form of a lesson or message.

Of course, it's much easier to just say, "Wow, what a coincidence!" But it's so much more fun to know that the people and events in your life are actually here for a purpose. Even better, they each have a gift for you. I love presents! But you have to watch out for them because these gifts have no bows or boxes.

As you pay attention to your world around you, you'll begin to understand the clues and hints and outright foghorn-messages that are right there in front of you. Those messages are working in sync and are here to help you create the life of your dreams. And admittedly, I have spent much of my adult life paying little attention. Holy cow, all those unopened gifts I left behind!

I look back on so many "coincidences" that I allowed to cross my path unnoticed. God spoke often, and so often I didn't listen.

Perhaps my growth would have been faster, and maybe my life lessons would have been richer. Thankfully, my God is patient and forgiving. He grins when I miss a valuable life lesson. He forgives when I chalk things up to accident or coincidence. Our loving God is quite fond of you and me, and for that, I'm humbly grateful.

My growing-up days were spent mostly with the neighbor kids three doors down. The King family had children about the same ages as ours, and so our families matched up well.

FIRST ON THE BLOCK

I'll always remember the day the Kings got the first color TV on the block. Uh oh, did I just date myself? And yes, for all you young whippersnappers, TV was black and white before it was color. And it was also big and bulky. And very heavy. And the picture was fuzzy. And the remote control? Typically, that was little brother (me).

What a memorable day that was, my entire family showing up at their back door, ready to witness the spectacle. And quite a spectacle it was!

It reminded me of the very first time I walked into the Houston Astrodome. My eyes just couldn't comprehend what I was seeing.

We all stood there, wide-eyed with jaws dropped. The impossible has been made possible! Sunday TV night will never be the same!

That's what your life is like after you FLIP IT and you start recognizing how everything around you has its reason and value for being here. It's literally a jaw-dropping revelation as life around you happens "on purpose." But you have to flip it. You have to come over to the other side and open your eyes to recognize the wonders happening all around you.

GOD'S VOICE

Did you ever wonder what language God uses or how He sounds? Stop long enough and notice everything going on around you. I believe His voice rings in many languages, from nature to accidents, from people's actions to movie lines. Even book quotes, rainbows, blossoms, sunsets, convictions, and your gut feelings; they are all ways God communicates to you. Yep, that word "coincidence" was invented by some jaybird who couldn't figure out the miracle. We feel a bit more in control when we can give it a name.

This has been one of the most electrifying FLIP IT choices I've made in my life. I'm talking about entertainment galore! What used to be a bunch of nothingness now makes sense. And I'm continuously filled with

> **Reminder**
> There are no coincidences, only Proofs of Alignment

anticipation, wondering who's next up. Who or what will enter stage right next and deliver my next adventurous lesson?

I'm a believer in God's metaphors. He created and positioned everything "on purpose." Look at the fruit at the end of the limb. It's always at the end.

Coincidence? Maybe. But I can share with you what it has taught me. In order to reach the fruit, I'll have to go out on a limb. I can't hug the safety of the trunk and reach the fruit. That stretching and risk-taking message is a clear reminder to me of what "faith" truly looks like.

And it has served me in making choices to act.

Have you noticed how every living thing expresses in some form? It "pushes out" and it lets go. From the air in your lungs to the sweat from your pores. From the shedding of the snake's skin to the tree's falling leaves. Everything alive expresses. And if it doesn't, it decays, implodes, or dies.

Two ears, one mouth? Good job on that one, God! His humor comes through loud and clear, telling me to listen twice as much as I speak. At least I'm giving it my best shot. *Honey, how am I doing so far?*

And what about the ebbs and the flows of the sea? And of your breathing? And the seasons? Everything ebbs and flows, in and out, in perfect rhythm. What a beautiful reminder that this too shall pass and that tomorrow's flow will surely follow today's ebb. Your life is a back-and-forth symphonic dance and promises to always bring you back home.

Reminder

Coincidence? or Divinely Purposed?

Have you noticed that growth is the evidence of life? Life is about growing, learning, expanding, progressing, ebbing, and flowing. Even a bicycle sitting still falls over. You and I are here on this earth, not to comfortably stagnate, but to move forward.

Your life is a movie, constantly revealing to you hints and secrets and hidden paths to the better life. How will you respond?

Bottom Line

Start replacing any dismissive judgments with curious questions. Consider how an event or emotion or spoken word or broken plan just might be giving you valuable insight or a new direction.

Begin holding life and all its events as a symphony with thought behind it. Look for the value in any circumstance, good or bad.

Sharpen your senses and flip your thinking. "By golly, this might be a God-Nudge." It's an adventurous and exuberant way to experience life, and this author highly recommends it!

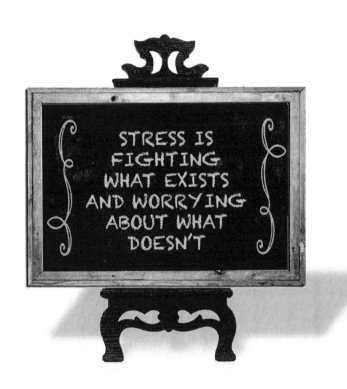

6

STRESSED?

FLIP IT!

THE STORY WE TELL OURSELVES

Stress is just a part of life. Hey, life is hard, I was wronged, he was stupid, they were at fault, and money is scarce. But it's nothing a bottle can't fix.

FLIP IT **Stress accelerates nearly 90 percent of all illnesses. The good news? It can be avoided.**

"Whenever I get stressed, I eat brownies, Blue Bell ice cream, and Dove chocolates. Why? Because stressed spelled backward is Desserts!"
— Anonymous

I positioned this chapter early in the book so we can attack it early. I believe stress is one of the most underrated killers of our mind, body, and dreams. What is stress anyway? It's easy to describe, but what exactly is it?

Stress isn't all bad, really. It can actually motivate you and me to prepare or perform better. That test or interview tomorrow needs you at your best. And that investment "hit" that your portfolio just took is prompting you to re-think your strategy. Stress can make you get the lead out!

Stress can even be a lifesaver in the face of danger. Pulse accelerates, breathing quickens, muscles tighten, your brain burns more oxygen...all hands on deck for survival!

Stress reminds me of a chocolate chip cookie. In small batches that cookie can be a good thing. But a consistent diet of those scrumptious little yummies, like a steady diet of stress, will eventually saddle you with more physical maladies than you bargained for.

Stress has conflicting definitions, but I think we can all agree on a few descriptions. "Pressure" hits home for me. I think I'm one of those "performs well under pressure" guys. Sometimes my stress sharpens my skills and my senses. But in larger doses, it destroys me! Some folks make a living performing under pressure. That's called chronic stress and that's the critter we want to avoid.

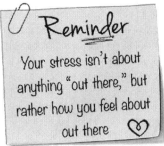

Reminder

Your stress isn't about anything "out there," but rather how you feel about out there ♡

Chronic stress looks like a lifestyle of GO-GO-GO! There's never enough time in the day and you never seem to have a moment to yourself. This is when those same life-saving responses in your body will begin to suppress your needed sleep, which affects your systems of immunity, digestion, and even reproduction. Yikes! And when those bodily functions start to malfunction, the doctor bills pile up. Sooner or later, you'll pay the big tab for that stressful lifestyle.

HERE'S THE GOOD NEWS

Even with that stressful pace, you don't have to be stressed. So, rather than succumbing to stress as a lifestyle, let's flip your thinking. I'm convinced of two truths about stress: It's a killer, and it can be prevented.

I'm well aware that some of you are experiencing some horrific stress right now. I respect and honor you.

Here's my definition: Stress comes from resisting what is and also from worrying about what is not.

I resist "what is" when I'm late to my appointment. I fuss and fight and push myself to get there quicker. But I'm going to be late and fighting it only has me arriving worn out...and late!

Resisting "what is" may have me all bunched up about the economy. But it is what it is. And no amount of my resisting what is will change it.

Resisting what is *not* looks like worrying about something that doesn't exist. I'm worried about their reaction to my opinion. I'm literally resisting something that does not exist.

Studies have found that stress increases the risk of many conditions such as obesity, heart disease, diabetes, depression, and even gastrointestinal issues.

Resisting what is; can it possibly be that simple? If you are currently feeling major stress in your life, I want you to stay with me here. We're going to do a little layer-peeling.

Bring to mind a current stress in your life. What's got your goat right now? It may be something with your job, your finances, your family. Let me take one guess at your answer: Your stress is over some part of life not going according to your plans. Something happened that wasn't what you think should have happened. Am I right? I'm a genius!

 Simply put, you are stressed because life didn't go your way, or you fear that it won't go your way, and you cannot be at peace with it. You are in resistance.

I find myself thinking, "But why did they do that? Why did she have to say that? I would have never done that! Why did that happen? That should not have happened!"

I cannot answer why things happen in my life. I can only choose how I will respond to what happened. But it's my trying to answer that first question of "why things happen" that keeps me in a stress rut.

Some may think, "Yeah, well, if you were just told that you had cancer, you'd be stressed too."

Perhaps I would. My place here is to remind you of what brings you more life and what depletes life. We're in this life together, my friend, and we're not getting out of it alive!

I watched my friend Byron grow visibly upset as he shared about his mediation proceedings with his soon-to-be ex. The mediation didn't go as he expected. He wanted to be granted more time with his kids. Otherwise, they would grow up delinquent, he was sure of it. He was visibly stressed with it all.

I saw standing before me an angry, defeated man. And he was spewing his anger toward the system and toward the mother of his kids. But in truth, his anger and upset stemmed directly from his lack of control. Life was not

Reminder

Whatever you make things mean is setting you up for internal stress or internal peace unfolding according to his plans and he did not like it one stinkin' bit.

Was the system right? Was it wrong? Was Byron right or wrong? It doesn't matter. What's important was his response to "what is." You and I have to ride life's pony, regardless of the path it takes. Simply put, you can ride it kickin' and screaming, or you can make the best of a ride you did not plan.

How effective can anyone possibly be while in that state of upset? His dukes were up as he helplessly and hopelessly poised himself against the world. He didn't stand a chance. I've never known anyone who beat the world, have you? Fighting life is like a boxer fighting air.

In his mind, his kids were going to be criminals and all mayhem was going to break loose, simply because things didn't go according to his plans. After all, *his* plans were the best plans!

Byron was resisting what exists, and at the same time, he was worried about what does not exist.

We've all been there. It's during that point of futility when we realize we just can't win and we have no control over the matter. Byron eventually made the choice that brought him more life and less strife. He resisted less, made peace with what is, which positioned him to deal with the matter productively.

When life doesn't deliver your own plan, then it's your move. You'll choose to work with it or against it.

This has nothing to do with surrendering to defeat, and everything to do with keeping your sanity so as to deal with life circumstances gracefully and effectively.

It's choosing to dance with life rather than to wrestle against it. That's what the great negotiators of our time have mastered. They accept who and what they are working with. Only then are they poised to work *with* them, rather than resisting against them.

Simply put, stress is your continued efforts to change the past or control the future. I have browsed and browsed and have found no one, not one human being, who has successfully changed the past. What's done is done! And stressing over something that no longer exists seems a bit empty, don't you think? You cannot change it, so let's figure out how to live with it.

HERE'S WHAT I FIGURE

For me, my best antidote against stress is my newfound power that comes through the choice of acceptance. In the state of stress, you're being held hostage by your own inner turmoil. And that turmoil is a product of your resistance. I'm sure it's no secret to you; your resisting is wearing you down.

NO STRING WAS FOUND

I have felt around my entire body and there is no string to be found. None. Not even a thread. There is no physical connection between what happens outside my body and what happens inside my body. My reaction to "out there" is 100 percent contrived by my thoughts! Not by "them or him or her or it." They were only the triggers to my thoughts.

Reminder

You will spend your days either fighting the waves or learning to Surf

"But wait a second, that's not right! My wife left me and you're telling me that it's my fault that I'm stressed?"

I said nothing about fault, shame, or blame. What you choose to feel and how you choose to think about it is entirely your choice, and no one else's. Your wife may have left you, but it's your choice to make it mean what it means. Your personal identity may have been compromised, but you and you alone are making it all mean what it means.

Now, this may seem unreasonable to you. I'm telling you that your choice to disagree or hate and resist is entirely your choice. But hold your horses, because this is actually good news. You see, if you hold the power to choose stress, then you also hold the power to choose peace or acceptance or forgiveness or empathy or faith.

YOU MAY HATE WHAT HAPPENED

You may resist what she said or didn't say or "what the hell he was thinking." I'm with you. But that internal resistance on top of more resistance is mounting and creating clogs that will someday catch up with you and deliver to you the bill.

When I blame my stress on my kids' behavior or my car accident or my wife's expensive shopping spree or that wacko client or those unscrupulous bill collectors, I am in effect handcuffing myself and telling life, "Take me! I'm yours! I surrender all power!"

 This is my favorite part of taking ownership of my stress. It's in owning your stress that you will no longer have to sit and wait for things or people to change or get better. Yes! You choose to make it mean whatever it means. The reality you create inside your head becomes your reality.

Is it really that simple? Yes, it is.

IT'S ALL IN YOUR HEAD

Let's not overcomplicate this. You really don't have to pay those high-priced shrinks to work you through this. Stress is in your head, in the form of pure and simple thought. Stress is not what happened or what should have happened or is fixin' to happen. Stress is your collective thoughts about it all. You pinned the definition on what it means, and then you chose to resist or not resist. And the longer you resist, just like in metallurgy, the more fatigued you'll become as you work toward your breaking point.

So how can you turn down the stress volume in your life? Well, I'm not going to pretend that I know your challenges and your degree of stress. And I honestly do respect your challenges and even your sorrows. But whether your circumstances are calm or chaotic, the same basic rules apply.

You must step outside yourself enough to objectively see your habitual reactions to people and things.

You've been doing it this way all your life, and so it may not be crystal clear at first. But it will serve you to objectively identify what it is in life that you are resisting.

DISEASE

Disease is the language your body uses to tell you that you have a need for emotional healing. When you are not at ease, you're at dis-ease. And when you're at war emotionally with something or someone in your life, then your body sooner or later displays that dis-ease in real-life form.

TRY THIS: Move, Express, Relax, Eat, Sleep, and Laugh.

- **MOVE**: Get up and get OUT. Exercise. Move your body. Physical activity helps produce your brain's feel-good neurotransmitters, called endorphins. That's why we feel better when we're on the move.

- **EXPRESS**: Holding things in too long will kill you; literally. Expression heals and repression kills. Practice telling your thoughts and feelings to a friend. Write your thoughts down in a journal. Sing them to your dog. If no one is there, do mirror-talk. My written journal is my lifesaver. I would not be here without it. Prescribe for yourself the medicine called "expressing."

- **RELAX**: Find a place where you can turn down the world's volume and just chill. You don't have time? Yes, you do. Nice try, though.

- **EAT**: Garbage in, garbage out. Cut down on sugars and processed foods and late-night grazing. And stop complaining about how hard it is. Respect your body as the God-given temple it is. Whichever way you are treating it now, it will eventually pay you back in full.

- **SLEEP**: Sleep is when your body quietly repairs your heart, blood vessels, and other organs. It's the pit stop for your race car. Sleep deficiency invites heart and kidney diseases, high blood pressure, diabetes, and stroke. If not now, eventually. So, if you're bragging about how little sleep you need, you're also declaring how much repair and restoration you are cheating and denying your bodily organs.

- **BELLY LAUGH**: There's no medicine available that can bring the healing power of laughter. That's how God designed us. Good job, God!

The above "things to do" will dramatically help your immediate stress.

But remember, you can't cure chronic indigestion with Tums. You can soothe your stress momentarily, but let's go for the permanent cure!

BOTTOM LINE ⌣

Get clear on who and what you are resisting, and then flip it. Flip your thinking and assign a different definition to what's really going on. The stress is in you, not in them. And your stress is caused by you, not by them. This will require demoting your ego from its throne. Your right to be upset and stressed needs to take a backseat to the happiness that you really want from life.

Practice responding differently to things and people when they don't line up with your expectations. Become less judgmental of their actions and more interested in your own need to resist their actions. Turn your frustration with "them" into fascination with yourself and your own upset.

Start letting go of your need to control their lives and their choices. Turn your focus on changing "in here" vs. trying to change "out there." And, in doing so, you'll begin experiencing more peace and happiness as you resist less. And in that state, you'll become so much more effective in everything you want to accomplish in your life as your stress gets out of the way.

**The world is your school ground to learn,
not your chess set to manipulate.**

In closing here (I'm getting stressed with this subject), I'll add my most effective and powerful action to the six listed above.

PRAY

Now, I'm not talking about reciting those words you memorized as a kid. And I'm not talking about telling God, once again, what it is that you need from Him. Just...pray. BE STILL and know that He is God. Be still in His presence, with gratitude and without agenda.

This may be different from what you've always thought about prayer. But I can assure you, learning to turn off your brain's motor and just "be" in God's presence will begin sanding down stress's sharp edge. Your circumstances may not go away, but you'll be much better equipped to work with them and through them, rather than against them.

Stress is resisting what is. Trying to change the past or control the future are two futile attempts that keep us bunched. LET GO. Let go of your need to control life. The more you let go and let life flow on its own course, the more you will be able to bask in the present. And remember, the present is where love lives.

7

HURRY UP
AND FAIL

THE STORY WE TELL OURSELVES

Risks are scary. They're just not worth the pain and loss. Besides, the life I have now is good enough.

FLIP IT Hurry up and fail! Holding back for fear of failing is keeping you from succeeding.

"Failure is not the opposite of success. It's a critical steppingstone TO success."
— Rob

Let's be loud and clear on this one. "Failure" is a common noun, not a proper noun. It is not who you are, it's merely a result of an action you might take.

Hey, Thomas Edison, how many times can you try and fail at creating the light bulb before you either call it quits or go insane? As for me, I may have lasted a dozen times. I would not have had the determination you had that kept you pushing through all those failures.

Thank God Thomas never saw that nine hundredth time of getting it wrong as the last straw or the final failure.

He told his critics that he didn't fail nine hundred times, but rather, he discovered nine hundred ways how not to make the light bulb. Now that's the mind-set of a champion. And it's that mind-set that kept his future path wide-open. I want you to adopt that mind-set.

Failure is a necessary part of success. And yet so many folks never leave the starting gate for fear they might fail. Condition yourself to include failures, big and small, as part of the journey. Start failing and fail often! Countless success stories began with failure.

Let's talk about baseball. Do you think the legendary Babe Ruth called his strikeouts setbacks? Do you reckon he became discouraged, depressed, or defeated while shouting obscenities at the pitcher? Not Babe. He was a pro. He called it what it was. It was a strikeout.

As much as the man abhorred striking out, my guess is that he gained value from each swing and miss. He probably learned a tad more about himself and his approach. Perhaps he learned more about the spin on the ball. Babe benefited from each loss by letting it expand his knowledge and skill set. And here's the ironic truth of it all: Babe Ruth wouldn't have been the successful legend he was if he had never swung and missed!

We learn through our mistakes, our mishaps, and our miscalculations. Rather than calling them bad, let's call them our teacher. Flip how you think about mistakes.

A superior baseball average is when a player fails to get a base hit two out of every three times. That two-for-three failure rate puts his batting average in superstar status.

Albert Einstein could not speak fluently before the age of nine. He later wrote, "Success is failure in progress." Michael Jordan came home after school one day in tears because the coach cut him from the school basketball team. Walt Disney was fired at an early age when his newspaper employer told him that he just wasn't creative enough. Imagine, Walt Disney lacking imagination? Bah!

Here's What I Figure

With each event or circumstance that looks like a setback, you have two choices before you. You can pick steppingstone, or you can pick roadblock. Your pick will largely determine your life's course. You and I are never the victim unless we choose that role.

I hear your wheels turning. You're thinking, how can divorce or a job loss possibly be a steppingstone?

When you allow those challenges to teach you and to show you the parts of yourself that need betterment, you're on the right track. But you'll need to plant that ego of yours in the backseat while you consider perspectives you may not have ever considered.

 Life is all about making new choices. And you can choose that setback to be a springboard instead of a pitfall.

My divorce was the classic example of the fork in the road for me. I was faced with the choice to get bitter or better. I was chompin' at the bit to choose bitter! She did and said things that burnt my toast. My mind was conjuring up all sorts of paybacks. But I still had a choice. And so do you, my friend, with each and every challenge or dilemma or loss or catastrophe you face.

My "failure" in marriage, coupled with my determination to better myself from it all, set me on a path that eventually led me to the healthiest, most fulfilling marriage that I always knew was possible. Thank you for saying yes, Franca!

What do you figure holds most folks back from success? What's the one thing that keeps us from living out our dreams and realizing our purpose?

Fear? Fear of what? Fear of failure?

So, let's have some fun here. What if you could never fail? What if, for this moment in time, failure was impossible, and success was guaranteed? If you could do or become anything you can imagine, what would that be? Go ahead, let yourself go there. Let yourself dream for just this moment. I'll wait...

I'm still waiting.

Did you always secretly want to be a dancer? A writer? A doctor? A musician? A missionary? A real estate agent? A pro athlete? Do you dream of starting that company or changing jobs? Come on, dream with me here.

We all have our secret desire. If you can't find it right now, that's OK. You just need to let yourself wander there in your mind. We keep ourselves from dreaming because our brain can't reason how we can possibly make money doing that. Or maybe we don't think that we're qualified, and so let's just avoid the pain of going there in thought.

Reminder

Failure will teach you things you could Never learn in school!

I have some good news for you. That one thing that you would secretly love to do or be is actually reachable! Yes, it is! And you can bet your bottom dollar that somewhere in this world, someone is doing it right now, and making a good living at it.

When you Flip this idea of failure, when you make it mean your steppingstone rather than your roadblock, everything changes colors. You'll begin to engage with people and things differently, which in turn will bring you new results. You'll make choices to move, whereas before, you refrained.

When you change your perspective on what failure really is, monsters look like mice and mountains look like hills. And as you instinctively take more action, you'll watch new doors open to your expanding world.

BOTTOM LINE ⌣

It's time to act. It's time to show the world that you are ready to flip your thinking on this failure idea. Failure exists; it's a vital part to success. There's not a successful person alive who has not failed.

**Live your life as if God has
stacked the cards in your favor.**

Imagine sitting at a poker table looking down at your newly dealt hand. Your heart stops as you stare at a Royal Flush! What? You're holding a Royal Flush! You immediately assume your poker face as your head rushes with anticipation.

Your palms sweat and your pulse quickens while you glance around the table trying not to give it away. Then you glance over at the dealer. As your eyes meet, he gives you a quick wink. He winked at you! Holy cow, the dealer winked at you! He stacked the deck, and it's in your favor!

My friend, that's your life. Your hand of life is stacked in your favor by the Maker Himself. That rough relationship you had years ago was preparing you for something better. It was teaching you the ropes. Did you pay attention? And to that loss, fear, or agony that you're experiencing right now, are you listening? That's the only catch; you have to pay attention and play out your hand. Oh, and don't worry, the dealer's got this.

Holding back is like staring at a Royal Flush in your hand, and telling life, "I pass." You must not hold back. No whimpering, pouting, blaming, settling for, giving up, excusing yourself, or buying the lie.

It's called Faith. It might not look like the faith you had as a kid. I'm not talking about the Sunday-morning-only variety. This faith is the Real McCoy. Gutsy faith. This faith feels the fear and does it anyway, because you know that life is calling you.

Reminder

You will make your Failure mean either a Stepping Stone or a roadblock, It's your call

Faith will have you taking a right turn even when your fears are telling you to cower to the left.

Remember, failure doesn't even exist, except in your mind. And so your thoughts are keeping you from succeeding.

Stop selling out to a fictional image. You have a world to conquer. There's no time to dillydally with such poppycock!

8

LET'S RELOCATE
YOUR UPSET

THE STORY WE TELL OURSELVES

If only everyone would cooperate with me and do the right thing! Of course, I'm upset! Look what the world keeps doing! Look how people keep doing stupid things!

FLIP IT   **Pinning your upset on someone else is like leaning your ladder against the wrong tree.**

*"Your upset is an inside job. Stop assigning it
to others and set yourself free to soar."*
— Rob

He looked down and yelled, "What did you say?" I yelled back, "You're not going to find any bananas up there! That's a pecan tree!"

Upset is a part of life. Indeed, it's a necessary part. It serves a purpose. It tips your applecart, trying to get your attention. Something needs to be healed, reconsidered, or rebooted.

But if you're like me, you've spent far too many hours barking up the wrong tree when it comes to upset.

My friend Bill Ferguson, founder of Mastery of Life, had a group discussion one evening. He asked a young lady in the room, "When you get upset, where exactly is your upset?"

She responded, "At my boyfriend, of course!"

Her "upset ladder" was leaning against the wrong tree. And when you're trying to resolve your issue of upset, while thinking that it's them and not you, you'll have more success trying to find that banana in the pecan tree.

Oh, and, by the way, her upset was and always is inside her, never anywhere outside of her. "Out there" is simply what triggers our upset "in here."

Here's What I Figure

Blaming others never took me to the root of my upset. It pushed it under the rug for the moment, which momentarily made me feel better. The upset has been stored inside me like a smoldering coal. I didn't know it and I could not see it, but when you poke that bear it comes out roaring! So naturally, I blame you, the poker!

My blaming others for my upset only kept me from facing any truth about myself and whatever issues I had brewing inside me. But my patient God just smiles and says, "Next time. Maybe you'll get it next time."

What if your upset isn't such a bad thing? What if it's actually something that serves you?

Upset is like the nerve endings in your skin. Are they bad or good? I mean, wouldn't it be great if we could just turn off the switch to those nerve endings so we wouldn't feel pain? Except, of course, for those times when you grab that hot pan on the stove. You know, the one that you forgot was still hot? It's a good thing your nerves alerted you that time. Or else, you would be having cooked hand for dinner!

Just like your nerve endings, your upset is a sounding alarm. Ding-ding-ding! What's that alarm about? I don't know, you tell me. I can assure you that whatever it's about, it has nothing to do with him or her or them or it. It has everything to do with you. And you're only hurting yourself by trying to silence the alarm.

I still prefer to avoid upset. I mean, who in their right mind wants to feel that emotion? I'm itchin' to share with you the good news I've learned about this because it will flip your perspective on virtually everything in your life.

We often schedule our very lives around avoiding upset or pain. I'll avoid making that phone call. I'll not ask her out for fear of being turned down. I'll not start that business; it's less scary to remain in the thinking/talking stage. I'll not RSVP to that party, just to avoid feeling uncomfortable with my body or my status or my inability to mingle. It's much more comfortable to stay home and fluff my pillow and pet my cat. Right, Bruno? There's no pain felt at home sweet home!

Reminder

Stop being a slave to your own upset! It's holding you hostage

So, what technique have you finely crafted in order to avoid feeling upset? Are you a fighter? A fixer? A fleer? Do you go zombie on us? Recognizing your choice of diversion is key to making new choices.

WHAT ARE YOU MAKING IT MEAN?

It's time to start reframing what you've been making your upset mean. It's gotten a bad rap. Life around you happens on your behalf to serve you, not to diminish you.

When you reframe that divorce or that accident or that tragedy, you then begin to understand that there's meaning and purpose in everything that has taken place. Even the most unbearable circumstance has some takeaway for you. Everything in this life is intentional and holds value for you.

There is no coincidence. When you get that, then you will no longer discount or dismiss what happened. No longer will any relationship or era or event be a waste of your time. You'll find the value and benefit from it.

Does your upset ever knock you off course? When I'm upset, my heartbeat races while my common sense escapes me. I call those moments "Boinks."

 Maturity defined: Finally understanding that life isn't going to play out according to my blueprint.

My friend, life is not always going to go your way, and people are not going to live according to your plans. So, give yourself a break and stop living from your reactions, and start living from your rational choices. Regardless of the chaos that you may feel right now inside, there's value in there for you, so pay attention and don't miss it. Growth seems to always require some form of upset to get it kick-started.

When you stop making your upset about them and start looking for the learning, you'll finally get to step off that treadmill and move forward!

Bottom Line ⌣

In that instance when you feel upset, STOP. Look in here rather than out there. Really get curious and fascinated with your own upset rather than offended or outraged with the thing that upset you. That out there is a dead end. Be still. Ask God for His insight. Be keenly open to whatever lesson or gem is being presented to you.

Listen, learn, grow, and prosper from it all. Class is in session so pay attention. Now, don't make me send you to the principal's office!

Reminder

Allow your Upset to take you within or you will go without

When you whittle it all down, your upset is really doing you a favor. It's telling you that maybe it's time to heal or make peace or let go or change or flip your thinking. What is it that your upset is telling you about you?

Always anticipate somewhere among those oysters is a pearl! I'm not talking about positive thinking or pie in the sky. Although, I will tell you that there actually *is* pie in the sky. I've seen it!

But I want you to catch yourself in the act of upset and practice choosing fascination over frustration. That's all it is: a choice! Your frustration will only stagnate the flow. But your inquiring curiosity will deliver to you the goods!

9

PROBLEMS?
NO PROBLEM!

THE STORY WE TELL OURSELVES

Problems are to be avoided at all costs! All they do is get in my way and hinder my plans.

FLIP IT **Quick-triggered judgment wants to call a person or event bad or unfortunate when we simply don't know the whole story.**

"I do not fix problems. I fix my thinking. Then problems fix themselves."
— Louise Hay

I grew up in a world of Little League baseball, Boy Scouts, capture the flag, and church youth groups.

Every day, about the same time, all household activities came to a halt. It was dinnertime, and nobody was to miss that sacred family ritual. I'm glad my folks taught us the value of eating dinner together. Those were special moments for us all.

I remember one of my favorite memories was when Mom took her famous Snickerdoodle cookies from the oven.

SNICKERDOODLES!

There's nothing like the smell of warm cookies coming out of the oven, am I right? My all-time favorite was the Snickerdoodle. That cookie offered the perfect combo of a soft center with a slightly crunchy crust.

Here's an interesting note about the Snickerdoodle cookie: The recipe requires an ingredient called cream of tartar. That's a white powdery substance you can find in your grocer's spice section. I can't tell you what it does, but it's a necessary part of the cookie dough.

One day, I wet my finger and snuck a taste of that mysterious white powder. Whoa! Yuck! Are you kidding me? That was some of the nastiest, most bitter stuff I had ever transported to my piehole. Nasty!

So, how do you reckon something so bitter can be used to make something so sweet? I never really gave it much thought until I became a big boy. Then it hit me: isn't that the very essence of life?

We are quick to dismiss what doesn't fit our narrative. It must be bad. And, if it's bad, then let's ignore it, shun it, or cut it off. It has no value here!

Many of us thought the recent COVID-19 shutdown was a bad thing. Every person had their individual story to tell. Some lost their jobs, their businesses, their marriage, their life. The world changed. Was that change good or was it bad?

HERE'S WHAT I FIGURE

Labeling it good or bad gets us nowhere. It was what it was, and those who embraced the changes are adapt and change for the better. Always anticipate change or "setback," and look for the blessings.

How many times do you reckon you've been protected by what could have otherwise been a tragedy? Your answer is you don't know. Because the tragedy never happened.

Thank God for everything, even for what didn't happen.

Reminder

We need challenges to prompt Growth. Where do we find challenges? FROM PROBLEMS!

You will face your problems with either a hateful or grateful attitude. Like it or not, the problem exists. It may not have been your preference, but it is your choice how you'll choose to hold it. How you respond will determine your life experience.

Don't allow the nasty taste of the cream of tartar to stop you from making the cookies. Make the darn cookies! And know that the process may require some "off" flavors at times.

Remember, a critical part of running a fine restaurant is stopping to clean the potties.

I've never seen a progress chart with a perfectly straight line. They seem to always resemble the shape of a staircase full of dips, drops, and what looks like setbacks.

I've had my share of dips and setbacks. At times, I have wanted to call it quits. And then I recall the cream of tartar story.

WHERE YOU ARE RIGHT NOW IS PERFECT

Keep in mind, it doesn't have to feel perfect to be perfect. At any moment, you are living out an important piece to a divinely orchestrated plan. Beware. Your shortsighted judgment can often lead to destructive reactions as you shut down, cut off, and burn connections.

I learned far more from my bad investments than I ever learned from my college accounting class. And that psychology class could have never seasoned me as well as my rocky relationships have.

In sales, we learn the SW-SW-SW-SW rule: Some will, some won't, so what? Some are waiting.

Make the shift. Reconsider how you respond to the "not so pretty" parts of life. Flip what you make the not-so-delicious things and people mean. Be more inclusive of what might not fit your blueprint. You'll eventually find that they are often here to make you better.

 Flip those judging thoughts into curiosity. Curiosity opens doors, and windows, and hearts, and possibilities, and it invites opportunities to heal.

You may not like what she just said, but let's try something new. Put a lasso on that ego, hold off on your judgment, and get curious for more clarity and more understanding. I can assure you, your desire to understand will take you much farther on your path than judgment or criticism. Proverbs 2:11 taught me the value of letting "understanding guard my heart."

KNOW THAT YOU DON'T KNOW

Know that you don't really know everything you think you know. Much of your "knowledge" is just your opinion. The devil's in the details, so stay open and willing and ready to surrender that urge to feel "in control." Trust me, God's vision for your life is much bigger and more thrilling than your vision will ever be!

Your life is like a symphony, my friend. Know that, at any given moment, a note might sound a bit "sour." But perhaps it's sour for good reason. And like the cream of tartar, those sour notes and strange flavors will someday show themselves as critical steppingstones in that masterpiece called "your life."

BOTTOM LINE

Let go of how you think your journey is supposed to look. Allow people and things around you to be different than what you expect of them. Don't confuse what looks bad, feels bad, and tastes bad with what's actually bad. Everything has its perfect place in your life, so grin and dance gracefully with the ebbs as well as the flows. That's what champions do best, and you are a champion!

> **Reminder**
> Problems always give us a chance to reconsider our values ♡

PART TWO

FLIP YOUR APPROACH TO LIFE

10

BE YOU, NOT
THAT OTHER YOU

THE STORY WE TELL OURSELVES

I can't be myself. In my relationships or at work. People expect me to be someone I'm not. Besides, who I am just might not be good enough.

FLIP IT This life is not a game of trying to be someone you're not, but rather, a journey of getting back to being yourself.

"Being you looks good on you! It's the best cosmetics your money can buy."
— Rob

We all want happiness. And in our wild goose chase to find it, life brings us full circle back to ourselves.

This is another one of those "things that we chase after but can never catch." Because it's not in the chasing that you will find your happiness. It's found in the process of getting back to yourself. Through the years we've all formed emotional barnacles that are holding our happiness hostage.

Have you ever traveled to an island or some faraway place and later came back home feeling energized and alive?

My wife and I love to go play at Disney World in Florida. My hope for everyone is to find the chance to go to that magical kingdom without kids! You heard me, without kids. Now, as much as I love my children, and had a blast taking them, that place is a playground for adults!

When I return home from Disney World, I feel like a million bucks. And I cannot wait to make a return visit there.

Why do you suppose we cannot wait to get back to that island or that mountain or that lodge in that remote forest? What was it about that vacation that made us feel so invigorated?

It wasn't the water. It wasn't the time off from the grind. And no, it wasn't the joy of sleeping late.

Reminder

BE YOURSELF.
It's the best cosmetics money can buy

And it wasn't the fresh air or all that exotic food. The aliveness and the joy that you felt was all about going to a place and time when you could just be you. And so you did. There was no pretense, no having to serve someone else, no need to perform, no "lost in the routine." You got the chance to just be 100 percent you, without concern or agenda.

Your sense of aliveness is found when you choose to BE YOURSELF. Being your authentic self brings you nose to nose with real love, real hopes and dreams, and a real connection to life itself.

"Oh, gosh no, trust me. I don't think the world wants to see the real me."

THERE'S NOTHING MORE ATTRACTIVE THAN THE REAL YOU

Authenticity is downright sexy, and you got it! Bring to mind that friend you admire. My guess is, that friend is genuine. Am I right? There's no facade, no pretense. And so you are drawn to them.

And conversely there's something quite repugnant about that other guy. You know, the one who's always putting on a show to impress. That's the guy who talks about himself and what he knows and what he's accomplished. He's not letting himself just "be," but rather he's "trying to be." He goes by the name Slick.

That acceptance and approval you're always trying to "get" from folks? You'll never get it by trying to get it. You'll get it by being your authentic self. You'll be like a magnet, attracting the affection of the "good guys" while repelling the bad ones.

Since way back during our diaper days, we've been told who we are and who we should be, and what we had better not become. "Don't be that way" or, "You could never be that." Sit there, think that, and, Lord have mercy, stop doing that! Crying is bad if you're a boy and good if you're a girl. Getting dirty is cute if you're a guy and bad if you're a little lady.

After being deluged with instructions and rules and social norms all my life, WHO THE HECK AM I?

I posed that question to one of my focus groups that I hosted in Houston. "Who are you"? After all, if the key to your happiness is found in being yourself, a good place to start would be knowing who you are.

"I'm an accountant," offered one person. "I'm a dad," said another. And from another, "I'm retired."

I responded to the group, "I didn't ask what you do or what your role is, I asked, who you are." It took a few attempts, but they eventually got there.

"I am grateful. I am present. I am loving. I am adventurous. I am curious. I am filled with marvel and anticipation. I am lonely. I am lost but hopeful." Everyone got the hang of describing what makes up who they are.

The "who are you?" question is a stumper because we've been so busy "doing" that we forget to "be."

 In your quest for happiness, you'll eventually find that happiness is experienced in that space in time when you choose to just be present with who you are.

Here are some popular cries heard from life's impostors:

"I just can't be myself in this relationship." Yes, you can. No one is making you be someone you're not. It's your choice. It always has been, and always will be.

"I can't be who I truly am at work. I'll get fired." Perhaps so. Why plant your tree in concrete? It cannot grow in concrete any more than a fish can survive in dirt. Clearly, happiness has much to do with your life being in alignment.

"People won't like the real me." That's your judgment and that's all it is. Remember, your fear of what might happen will often hasten its arrival only because you fear it will. Never let your fear of what *could* happen make nothing happen.

"I can't be honest with him." Yes, you can. You are holding back because of your desire to control an outcome that's not your business to control. Let your truth set you free, and let it set your relationships free to get off the fence and either dissolve or grow.

In a world of making choice after choice to project or speak or think or to be someone other than who we truly are, we've forgotten who we truly are! And yet the ultimate key to happiness is to live out your authentic self.

We are bombarded daily with messages that keep us living in the "someday" rather than in the present. The world tries to sell us on something "out there" that will bring us the "in here" joy we are looking for.

Here's What I Figure

Rumor has it, when the artist Michelangelo finished carving the now-famous statue of David, someone asked how he was able to carve such an intricate piece of art from a solid slab of stone. He replied, "It's easy. I just chiseled away the parts that didn't look like David."

A PLANT-LOVING PRINCIPAL

The assistant principal of my son's middle school was one of the hardest working folks I've known. Cynthia's work ethic always landed beyond what was required of her. But behind her empty smile, I saw a woman without passion. Her work had slipped into the repetitive mindless task mode.

One morning I invited her over for coffee. I asked her what she loves most in life. After a few attempts to get past the typical pat answers, she was able to share with me what truly lit her up. And surprisingly, her answer had nothing to do with kids or education!

Reminder

Pure Freedom is choosing to be Yourself

Imagine that, an assistant principal whose love for kids wasn't even close to the top of her list.

She told me how she loved growing plants and working with the earth. She especially loved growing flowers. As she shared, I watched her face light up. She became more and more expressive and animated. It was as if someone flipped a switch and she came alive, right there in my sunroom.

I asked, "If your passion is in plants, why don't you pursue that for a living?" I'll bet you can guess her reply. Or rather, her objection.

"I can't make money tending to plants."

My goodness, this world has successfully lulled us all into being and doing things that aren't really "us," hasn't it? Now, there's certainly nothing wrong with a plant lover working at a school. And there's nothing wrong with whatever profession you've chosen for yourself. That is, if your job or career hasn't sucked the life right out of you while numbing your dreams.

All I could do was remind her of what she most loved and valued in life, and then encourage her to not neglect or forget her passion.

Fast-forward fifteen years later. I received a note from Cynthia, updating me that she had moved out of the city and was now working for a plant nursery. She was finally doing what she loved and was happy as a clam.

My friend, your aliveness and your joy are not found in anything or anyone or anywhere other than right there inside you. It's been there all along, and you've simply been dancing circles around it, in search of it.

You avoid being yourself, for fear that who you are doesn't cut the mustard. On some level, you believe that you're not enough to be successful, or to keep quality friends, or to feel content and fulfilled.

Here's an irony for you: In your struggle to keep your friends or your happiness, you lose yourself in the process.

BOTTOM LINE ⌣

Be about the business of unlearning and undoing those things in your life that don't look like you. It's inventory time! Like Michelangelo, identify what's you, and start chipping away what's not you. This might look like choosing new friends or activities or hobbies or habits or even career.

Franca and I recently stepped back and looked at the people in our lives. We thought about who adds to our journey and who detracts. There's a bit of truth to the old saying, "You become who you hang with." It's important that you hang with those who respect and even share your values and ethics.

I'm not suggesting you cut folks out of your life. But now and then there comes a time to relocate a few of them from your inner circle to your less-intimate outer circle of friends. Choose your friends "on purpose."

WHAT DO YOU LOVE?

I want you to take five minutes out and list all the things in life that you *love*. Fill up the page. Then on another page list those things in life that you *value*. That might look like family, honesty, adventure, security, etc. Those two pages will give a good description of the real you. Now, begin chipping away those activities, things, and people in your life that don't align with these descriptions.

What you'll find, as you begin this journey back to you, is power. There's newfound abilities and confidence when you stop playing the game and begin living your truth. Life will take on a refreshing zeal as you find deeper joy and love and aliveness within yourself, and for other people.

Remember, God crafted you to be you, my friend. So, get out of your own way and get back to being you! You'll then see life around you start to click on all cylinders.

 As you get back to you, your world around you will miraculously begin to support the new (original) you.

11

YOU HAVE NO SOUL

THE STORY WE TELL OURSELVES

I sometimes feel like I have a soul. But that's a religious thing, isn't it?

FLIP IT Your body is here to support and transport you. You ARE your soul.

"The components of life that are real cannot be seen with your eyes, but with your soul."
— Rob

What are you? What part of you is you?

Are you your brain? That's where your thoughts are, right? So, is that you in there? But wait, how can you be your brain if the real you at times *controls* your brain? Then, who is the "you" who's doing all that controlling?

What are you?

Maybe you are your heart. That's what keeps you alive. And we talk about "following your heart" all the time.

Or maybe you are a combination of both heart and brain? But wait. When you die, and those body parts decompose, does that mean that you yourself will decompose as well? Yikes!

Have you ever noticed that the most important parts of life are the things we cannot visibly see, touch, or smell?

"But wait! You mean apple pie isn't real?"

Oh gosh, apple pie is real all right! Put a scoop of my favorite Blue Bell brand Vanilla ice cream on the side and it becomes more real! But don't get me started.

So, here's the scoop. Those things in your life that you can see and touch will eventually rust, wilt, melt, break, get outdated, be stolen, or die. Your tennis racket, egg salad, and those sexy britches you're wearing—they will all go away someday.

And those things that you cannot see, touch, or smell are eternal. No one can ever take those from you, nor will they ever rust, wilt, melt, break, get outdated, be stolen, or die. And the best part? None of them cost more than a dollar. What a deal! I'll take a dozen!

Those precious invisibles of life, among others, are love, joy, peace, hope, vision, humility, forgiveness, your soul, and your God who created it all. The other physical things are just props positioned here to get you around and help you expand and live out your life on this earth.

I was raised in a small Methodist church nestled in a suburban Houston neighborhood. My parents took us to church every Sunday morning. I was a fidgety lad who could think of better uses of my time, such as throwing a baseball or shooting cans with my pellet gun.

During the church service, they talked about our souls going to heaven after we die. So then, are you your soul? If so, where is the soul located? My guess is somewhere behind the kneecap, but I'm probably way off.

Here's What I Figure

We are not people who have a soul. We ARE souls. And so contrary to what you'll see in the tabloids, you are not your body. That body of yours is basically a taxicab here to wheel your soul from spot A to spot B.

During the years when I viewed others as "bodies with souls," my thoughts and conversations were primarily on the physical plane. Chitchat was relatively superficial. "How are you doing? Fine, how are you? Fine thanks."

I once judged people by their appearance and their words and actions, not giving much thought to that invisible force that was driving them. But I flipped it! And I'm still flipping it. You can't turn a barge in an instant and you can't change old habits overnight. But I have noticed an entirely fresh new spin on life as I now see through the eyes of my soul vs. through just my eyeballs. And I like what I see.

Reminder

We are not humans having spiritual moments, we are Spirits having a human moment

HERE'S YOUR BONUS

There's benefit to seeing others as souls with bodies vs. bodies with souls. Rather than living in reckless judgment of what you see, you'll be open to the person's invisible underlying truth. Rather than staying in anger at someone's action, you'll look beyond the obvious and see his pain.

A businessman was on his routine drive home one day. Suddenly, a rock flew up from the deep roadside ditch, shattering his windshield. He came to a screeching halt, slammed his door behind him and made a beeline to the ditch. He yelled, "Where are you, you little punk! Come outta there right now!"

As he approached the edge of the ditch, he found a kid, all right. But it wasn't what he expected. Lying there, painfully trapped beneath his bike, was a child desperately trying to get someone's attention.

When your vision extends beyond the physical realm and considers what your eye cannot see, then you're cookin' with gas! What people are wearing or doing for a living is second to wanting to know and understand "who they are."

What a freeing way to engage with the world around you! You'll pass a stranger you've never met and find yourself blessing him or her in your thoughts or with a smile. You'll see that homeless person on the corner as a hurting child, rather than merely judging them for their bad choices.

BOTTOM LINE 〰

Look past the words, attitudes, and actions of others and begin seeking to understand the source. See the visible and seek the invisible. I like to call it empathetic listening.

You've surely experienced times in your life when you were suffering and trying desperately to make sense of things. Practice giving others that right to suffer or to be in pain or to feel lost. Allow them their own path.

You can't truly know the anguish that your ex is experiencing. You can't know how the guy who cut you off feels about himself after losing his job or fighting with his wife. You just can't know. But you can decline judgment and choose empathy and forgiveness. And in doing so, you'll feel the freedom from toxic judgment.

Flip what you have made people in your past mean. They were not here by accident. They are souls, each of them, and they were perfectly positioned where they belonged. Everyone, past and present, is a purposeful part of your spiritual journey. Yes, I said spiritual. Because that's what you are. You are a spirit. A soul. That's the only part of you that will not die. That's...you.

Wake up! Start witnessing the most amazing spectacle ever...the spectacle of the invisible world and all of its driving forces and emotions. Best of all, you'll begin recognizing miracles happening all around you!

You don't *have* a soul; you ARE a soul. And everything of the soul is real and is free. If you can see it, buy it, drive it, or put BBQ sauce on it, then it's temporal and here to help you, teach you, transport you, feed you, and grow you.

12

YOUR UGLY SIDE
IS YOUR
ATTRACTIVE SIDE

THE STORY WE TELL OURSELVES

To be successful I must present my polished self. I cannot let my guard down and be real. Vulnerability shows my weakness.

FLIP IT When you hide your authentic and genuine side, you hide your Power. Vulnerability IS power.

"You'll impress me by your strength,
but you will win me over through
your weakness."
— Rob

We guard ourselves against being vulnerable, yet our vulnerability will attract the very things we want.

Michael Jordan will go down in history as one of the most talented and revered pro basketball players in the game.

I remember when he was inducted into the NBA Hall of Fame in 2001. The audience greeted him with a standing ovation as he came forward to give his enshrinement speech. Michael stood there, humbly taking in the moment.

THEN CAME THE TEAR

A tear shot down his left cheek. And the instant he reached up to dry it from his eye, the crowd's applause crescendoed into a frenzy. The man showed his humanness. He exposed his down-home vulnerability, and the world responded with grace and endearment.

I've lost count how many times I've heard, "You must stay strong." You hear it at funerals, weddings, and any event that begs you to show emotions. Back when I was filming weddings, I often heard a bride chastising her dad for crying! Now and then a mom would brag to me after the ceremony, "At least I didn't cry."

What is this! What's wrong with us! We're consumed with trying to hold it all together. Let's not dare show any sign of "weakness." Be strong and look polished.

This trick we all learned, this technique of only showing our sparkling shiny side, ironically undermines the thing that we all want most. We want connection with others. That's how we're wired. We thrive on personal connection, and yet we prevent real connections from happening with our cool, calm, and collected selves.

While we are preoccupied with appearing flawless, we literally keep amity at an arm's distance.

As I hosted focus groups, I saw many moments when the display of weakness melted the crowd. Jack had the floor one night. And the more he shared, the more his face conformed to the painful recollection of his past. And then came the tear.

I remember the complete shift of synergy in the room that very second a tear fell. From that moment on, each of us felt an instant connection with Jack.

Bring your strong, guarded self over here and sit next to me for a minute. It's time we talk about this meaning you've given to this word "strength."

Here's What I Figure

It never occurred to me how much depth was missing in my relationships until I began offering up more of the "real" me. You know, the me who feels fear, doubt, and emotions, and is willing to show them. But, to do so I had to give up that sense of feeling in control. To show my vulnerable side I had to let go of my need to make sure they like me or accept me.

Reminder

Your Vulnerability Invites Connection

It tuckers you out, trying to make sure the world only sees the perfect side of yourself. And yet, it takes no effort at all to let go and just be yourself. And when you do, folks will receive you with grace and affection. And those who don't, just remember the adage: Those who matter don't care, and those who care don't matter.

Showing your imperfections and humanness will bring you more quality connections and genuine friendships.

THE KEY TO VULNERABILITY

Find the courage to let go of who you think you should be. That's only keeping you living an illusion while depriving the world of your God-made authentic self. What a travesty! This world wants and needs you, not that other you that you think you're supposed to be.

**Your fantasy of who you *should*
be is not real. Don't live the lie.**

Vulnerability doesn't come overnight. After all, you've been perfecting that snazzy, sparkly, cover-up of yours for years. But you can certainly start now by making a few choices to show your cards.

C'mon now, I didn't write this book for your entertainment. I want you to make a new choice right now. Just one. How do you eat an elephant? One bite at a time.

BOTTOM LINE ㄴ

Flip those moments when you have the opportunity to let your hair down. I think you'll be pleasantly surprised by the new results your new choices will induce. Folks will like you when they can relate to you, and we all relate to down-home bona fide sincerity.

Here, I'll go first: So, I was talking on my cell phone not long ago, rushing around the house, collecting things so I could dash out the door. I was blabbering away while canvassing the house with my eyes, becoming more and more frustrated. Why was I

Reminder

You might impress folks with your "perfect side," but you will win them over with your Real side

frustrated? Because I couldn't find my cell phone. Yep, you heard it right. I was on my cell phone looking for my cell phone. OK, did I just share too much?

Perhaps you can relate to these moments that give you the invitation to show your real McCoy-self:

🖖 Choose to say "I love you" first, rather than holding back for fear of looking stupid or feeling naked.

🖖 Choose to call up a new acquaintance and tell them that you're really looking forward to their friendship, despite your fear that they may not respond.

🖖 Choose to feel the fear of what the doctor's post-scan report will be. Surrender to the notion of unwelcome news.

🖖 Choose to give a relationship your all, rather than holding back for fear that it may not work out.

🖖 Choose to ask the "stupid" question in the room, regardless of what others may think of you.

🖖 Choose to tell your close friend that you feel lost in life, and that you just don't have it all together right now.

🖖 Choose to say, "I was wrong, and I am sorry."

🖖 Ask someone for their help, feedback, or input.

There's power, clarity, and likability when you choose to put your humanness on display to the world. That acceptance and love you've always wanted will come to you like white on rice when you put down your performance cloak and present to the world around you your authentic, adorable self.

13

YOU'LL SEE IT
WHEN YOU BELIEVE IT

THE STORY WE TELL OURSELVES

I said it all my life...I'll believe it when I see it. Show me the goods and I'll bite. Meanwhile, I'll just sit right here and not take any risks until you prove that I'm safe.

FLIP IT Your stone-hard belief that you will see it is what will make it so.

"Faith is acting like God
is telling you the truth."
— Rob

In your life, you're either waiting for assurance, or you are assertively stepping into the unknown with a sense of knowingness.

My favorite state slogan is from the Lone Star State: "Don't Mess with Texas."

I also like New Hampshire's slogan, "Live Free or Die." Oh yeah! Bring it on!

The state of Missouri puts its slogan on the license plates: "The Show-Me State." Can't fool those guys. They need proof!

We've all heard the expression, "I'll believe it when I see it." There's a doubting Thomas in us all, I reckon. I want to introduce you to a new spin that I think will change your life.

Here's What I Figure

Faith is acting like God is telling the truth. When He tells you that He will "never leave you or forsake you," or, "All things work for the good for those who love Him," that's a humdinger of a promise!

THE POWER OF YOUR BELIEFS

Your inner beliefs overpower your sweat-efforts every time. If you think you'll fail, then that belief will have a sabotaging effect on your best efforts. Try as you may, your beliefs will dictate making or not making that phone call or sales call. Your fear (belief) that you won't succeed will undermine your every decision and action, so as to ensure that you're right.

You were created with every tool you need to accomplish great things. I contend that your life circumstances right now say less about your skills and abilities and more about your thinking process. So, what do you say we do a little Flipping?

Reminder

FAITH is a Knowingness without needing proof

You formed a set of beliefs when you were a little guy or girl. Your beliefs about money, love, time, God, friendships, marriage, dating, and life itself—they are still with you. All your beliefs, many that you formed way back then, are now playing a guiding role in your everyday actions.

BOTTOM LINE ⌣

Let's put your beliefs on the table and do a little reassessing. Although you and I are limited by our beliefs, thankfully we have the freedom and the power to change old beliefs, as well as to choose new ones.

YOU'LL SEE IT WHEN YOU BELIEVE IT

The first step to having success or favor is believing that it's possible. You must believe that it's yours for the taking. If you want to heal, then know that you are healed! Do not wait to see your healing. Envision it so strongly that you are already giving thanks for it before it arrives. What you desire is already here. Time simply hasn't yet caught up with it.

In which part of your life are you holding back? Your marriage? Your business decisions? Your job performance? Your parenting? Your friendships? Your spiritual walk? Your life's direction? What would your life look like if you truly, truly know that God's got your back and that He really does have a more abundant life in mind for you?

Reminder

FAITH is taking that first Step when you can't see the whole Staircase

What would your relationship with your wife or husband be like if you didn't guard yourself, but instead, let yourself love fully and unconditionally? What would your business look like if you knew that it's truly bigger than you and that you simply need to get out of your own way? What would your life look like today if you had not held back and remained indecisive? How would you feel if you chose to shed your judgment and forgive?

Believe it, act on it, and then you'll see it. Know that what you want is there. Believe it so strongly that you can see it, smell it, and taste it. Then your actions will rise up and you will meet no insurmountable contention.

14

PAIN IS GAIN

THE STORY WE TELL OURSELVES

Are you insane? Who wants pain? I sure don't! Life is about pain-free comfort. Now, will someone please come fluff my pillow? Thanks.

FLIP IT Avoiding pain typically ensures a repeated lesson. And nobody likes to stay in after school! Face your pain, see its purpose, and graduate.

> *"Life is a classroom. Let me introduce you to your teacher, Mr. Pain."*
> — *Rob*

Pain is inevitable, but misery is optional. And continually avoiding pain will set you up for eventual misery.

Find pleasure in pain? Have I lost my marbles? Am I suggesting that we actually *like* pain? How can there possibly be any semblance of joy in a painful situation?

THE COCOON

A young boy was exploring in his backyard when suddenly something caught his eye. On a lower-hanging branch above his head, he noticed movement. He squinted in search until his eyes landed on a tiny cocoon. The little shell was shaking and wiggling! He soon realized that there was a newly formed butterfly inside, struggling to break free.

The boy dashed back to the house, grabbed a pair of scissors off the kitchen counter, then off he went to the rescue. He carefully cut a slit in the lower third of the pod, then gently shook the branch to help loosen the butterfly from its captivity.

The butterfly quickly fell out of the cocoon and straight to the ground. What? It didn't fly! The boy tried and tried to make the butterfly take its first flight. It never happened.

The butterfly was robbed of the critical last stage prior to emergence. The struggle and effort it takes to bust through and emerge are necessary to develop the flight muscles. And so, what looked like a rescue attempt was no rescue at all.

Pain is not only a part of the game, it's a necessary part.

Tony Robbins explores how we've each designed our lives around avoiding those things that we've deemed most painful. You and I dodge and avoid unpleasant experiences, sometimes unknowingly. Our lives resemble the babbling brook that winds its way down the hill, twisting and turning to avoid those hard rocks.

> **Reminder**
> See your pain as one of those crazy, wacky flailing-arms guys just trying to get your attention

VIKTOR FRANKL GAVE THE WORLD A GIFT

His indescribable torture in a Nazi prison camp during WW II left Viktor Frankl with little choice. He watched his comrades around him die off one by one, but he somehow rose above it all. He made a choice that didn't allow his environment to swallow him up. Frankl showed the world that, no matter how horrific your life circumstances, it's your thinking that gives you the overriding power.

Frankl wrote, "Life is never made unbearable by circumstances, but only by lack of meaning and purpose."

He witnessed this firsthand, as some of the Holocaust survivors were able to make it through the ordeal by connecting to a sense of purpose. Frankl claims that man's spirit can rise above his surroundings. "When we are no longer able to change a situation, we are challenged to change ourselves," he wrote.

Now, if Frankl could make sense of what I believe was one of this world's most horrific and painful times, then I can surely make sense of my business downturn or my lost credit card or my sprained ankle or failed relationship.

We tend to treat pain like the weed in the yard that has no value to us. And yet we know better. Our gym workouts are meaningless without pain or discomfort. Those muscles have to break down before they can build back.

HERE'S WHAT I FIGURE

In past relationships, I mastered the art of fleeing. When the conversation got too dicey, I went MIA. Working in my garage was far less painful than dealing with an angry woman!

But that was like eating a candy bar to soothe my sadness. It feels great in the moment, but it catches up with me sooner or later. And so, obviously, my avoiding those painful conversations led to isolation within the relationship. And after a few years of the same choices I found myself married to a stranger.

What is life, if not growth? When you and I are not growing and expanding, then we're slowly dying. Although growth is often kick started from a good book or sermon or a new thought, accelerated growth seems to always be predicated by some sort of discomfort, pain, or pruning.

I like to call them boinks. You know, those little jabs, pokes, pricks, and pains you feel when life doesn't go your way? A boink occurs when someone pushes your button. From a relationship ending to a business crashing...Boink! Ouch!

CHAMPS AND CHIMPS

Here's what separates the champs from the chimps. When that boink hits, you get to choose how you reply. You'll either react or you'll respond.

Reacting looks like resisting, fighting, fleeing, denying, ignoring, or medicating. And that will only buy you a ticket back to the end of the line to do it all again. If you didn't get the lesson this time, you'll always get another shot at it later.

You can also choose to *respond*, which will keep you engaging and learning. Now you're cookin' with gas!

Reminder

We mature with Damage, not with Years

Consider, for a moment, what if pain is an intentional part of life? What if it's here to serve you? What if, in an odd sort of way, your pain is God's way of knocking you off your saddle for your own good? Always remember, life isn't happening TO you, it's happening FOR you. And I suggest that pain is desperately trying to get your attention.

98

Your pain may be trying to help you bring closure to a part of your past. One of the most debilitating choices you can make is to drag your unresolved past issues into your present. And when you avoid emotional pain, you're saying no to healing and closure that you desperately need to move forward.

When you ignore issues and blame others, you're making your "next pay for your ex."

Let me explain. If you didn't learn your lessons in your past broken relationship, you will probably carry those same unresolved issues into your next  one. Your next relationship will then pay the price for your past ones. Own your stuff and graduate!

I've been able to make peace with the death of my big brother through countless moments of healing. Each time I attended a funeral, I mourned a bit deeper for my own loss. Sometimes a movie or book would trigger that old pain that helped me heal just a tad more. When you shed a tear for someone's sorrow, many times it's a tear for your own past sorrow. So, don't fight it. Expressed grief heals.

God puts frequent opportunities in your path for healing and closure. Don't brush it off or avoid it. You need it to help you feel it, heal it, and seal it. You can then catapult higher with your lighter spirit. Doors open after you've closed those that needed closing.

Reminder
Every Pain has Gain on its coattail, but you may have to seek it out

Viktor Frankl was literally writing his story with each and every excruciating daily choice he made to keep breathing.

He found his meaning and today, years after his death, he is helping the world cope with tragedy through his testimony and his work.

When you reframe your divorce or accident or tragedy or setback or failure, you'll gain an entirely new perspective. When you insist that it's useful and with purpose, you'll gain power through insight.

Don't take the "poor me" bait. That victim mind-set will remove you from the power you'll gain from owning it.

Remember, everything holds value. Nothing happens in this life void of meaning. And when you accept this, you'll begin to see things you've never seen before! You'll even recognize miracles!

I honor whatever pain you may be experiencing right now through your loss, abuse, or disorientation. And you certainly need to move through the grieving process at your own pace. Please keep in mind, regardless of the chaos you feel right now, there's gain waiting for you on the other side of your grieving. I don't believe God is in the business of causing pain in your life, but He certainly can turn any pain into some form of beneficial gain.

Be still and ask God for insight. Look for the opportunity to listen, learn, grow, and even prosper from it all.

BOTTOM LINE ⌣

Insist on making lemonade from those lemons! You are designed for bodacious prosperity and accomplishments. Do not faint in the face of pain, and always find the good in what appears bad.

See pain not as discomfort but as a necessary nudge to advance you. Make less resistive choices with your emotional pain. Stop denying, avoiding, or medicating, and start asking the important questions. Be still and work through your emotional pain rather than skirting around it. The only route to the other side is moving smack-dab through your pain.

 Remember, pain is like your shadow. You will never outrun it. The only way to shake it is to stop running, turn around, and shed light on it.

"What don't kill you makes you stronger." Yep, that old adage is true. Your fear of pain is keeping you from growth, and growth is life. God made you with the ability to withstand the pain. You can do this. So, ride that pony, because it's here for you to ride. Let's go!

15

HABITS AND
ADDICTIONS

THE STORY WE TELL OURSELVES

Overcoming a habit or addiction is grueling. It takes dedication, sweat, diligence, and struggle. Losing weight or beating poverty is going to be a grind.

FLIP IT Your superpower will emerge when you get busy being yourself, rather than trying to be who you *wish* you were.

"You'll dance much easier if you take off those boxer's boots and put on those dance slippers."
— Rob

Fighting an addiction can become the fight of your life. I want you to consider flipping your entire approach.

You may be wrestling with overeating, smoking, alcohol addiction, or poverty. And I will not pretend to know your anguish. I've seen up-close the sweat and tears that go into such battles, and I've noticed a common vein in all of them. I see a mind-set that may be setting you up for failure from the start.

I've always been motivated by the "why not?" questions. John Kennedy crafted his own rendition of an old George Bernard Shaw expression. He said, "Some men see things as they are and say, why; I dream things that never were and say, why not?"

Trying to flip your behavior is one thing. But when you flip your base-thinking, that's a whole new ballgame.

EVEN YOUR DOG KNOWS THE ANSWER!

So, why does a dog bark? Because he's a dog! And why does a rabbit hop? Because it's a rabbit. And that, my friend, is key to helping you overcome any substance battle.

Now, stay with me. I promise you, all the answers to complicated issues are simple. And this one is no exception.

When you're struggling to lose weight, your struggle comes from trying to become something that you believe you are not. "I'm fat, but I want to become something else."

Whenever you try to become someone you're not, It's a struggle. It's an uphill battle. When you see and define yourself as a fat person, then losing weight becomes a battle against your belief. Your belief faces off against your desire , and so guess which one wins the battle? Which one has the upper hand, your desire or your belief? Go ahead, I'll give you one guess.

Beliefs win out every time.

"But I AM fat!"

So you may be. Hang on to that and let's get to the core. For this conversation, I want to eliminate the words "habit" and "addiction." If you smoke, let's just say that you smoke. Somewhere along the path you determined you are a smoker, and therein lies the answer. At some point in time, you made the leap in your mind that took you from "I smoke" to "I'm a smoker."

You might be saying, "But I AM a smoker!"

If you see yourself as a smoker, then becoming something different will be a fight. Acting against your belief is counterintuitive and counterproductive. It's just a life rule.

Try this alternative on for size: You are a nonsmoker smoking a cigarette.

What's the difference, you ask? The difference is like night and day. One is powerful, and the other is powerless. One refers to "what you are doing" and the other refers to "who you are."

Reminder

Whatever you Focus on Expands

Hang with me, this is getting good.

So, here's a question for you smokers: Were you born with a cigarette in your hand? Of course not. You know why? Because you're not a smoker. And here's a question for my obese friends: Were you born obese? Of course not. So, "who you are" is *not* obese. And you must not define yourself as such.

You are a healthy love-machine who is momentarily overweight, rather than a fat person wanting to change.

You are a nonsmoker holding a cig, rather than a smoker wanting to change.

However you choose to label yourself is going to greatly influence your path. You will be what you will be, because your thinking makes it so.

Try, try, try as you may. Therapy, alternatives, and cold-turkey attempts may temporarily end your addiction. But when the dust settles, your life is a screenplay, and you are acting out what you deep-down believe about yourself. Changing your belief will naturally prompt a change in behavior.

Here's What I Figure

If you have defined yourself as a poor man from the poor side of the tracks, there's a good chance you'll stay poor. It's no wonder that 70 percent of lotto winners end up broke within a few years. A poverty mind-set, no matter how big the win, will eventually steer you back to poverty.

STOP TRYING TO QUIT SMOKING

You'll begin doing the things that nonsmokers do when you truly see yourself as a nonsmoker. Until then, your efforts will come from struggle.

What do nonsmokers not do? They do not smoke. Your inward beliefs always figure out how to manifest themselves into your outer world. I'm well aware of the chemical imbalance argument, and I am not suggesting that kicking the habit is easy. I'm telling you that the bumps are significantly lessened when you flip your thinking before you tackle the cause. This is a classic example of "work smart not hard."

 What are you striving for in your life? Do you want to be self-employed? How badly do you want it? So badly that you have convinced yourself that's who you are? When it becomes "who you are" rather than what you wish for, then any and all obstacles will transform down to mere road bumps.

**Obstacles are no match
for a firmly held belief.**

Do you want to lose weight? Then take yourself back in time when you were that hunk-o-beauty. There! Right there! That's who you are. See yourself as that. See your gorgeous trim self so clearly that you start naturally doing the things fit folks do.

Why? Because that's who you are! Your diet and exercise will come more effortlessly because that's who you are. It will no longer be a game of struggling to become someone you're not.

This is one of those "I'll see it when I believe it" principles. I want you to put as much work into your thinking as you do into your physical efforts and exertions.

Bottom Line

I assure you that whatever you hold in your mind as being true will eventually prove itself in the physical realm.

I'm a big fan of positive thinking. But positive thinking alone is somewhat baseless. Start on first base, start with cultivating your belief that will support that positive thinking and your desired outcome.

Repeat after me, all you smokers out there: "I no longer smoke because I am a nonsmoker." I want you to rear back your head and laugh at such a silly notion that you are a smoker! It's nonsense! There, now, doesn't that feel more like it?

All you larger folks out there, c'mon and say it with me. "I honor and respect my body because I am fit, I am healthy, I am sexy"! Those words will take on power as they become your core belief about yourself.

Your thoughts, words, and actions reflect what you truly believe. So FLIP IT! Flip your belief!

Tired of your addiction? You should be. That's not how you came into this world and it's not who you are. And when you truly step up to the plate and get the power of your beliefs, you'll harness that power in your favor. You'll shake off the shackles and scream to the world, "Enough!"

I've witnessed many in my circle who have been successful with this. And, unfortunately, I've seen a great number of people still in the trenches, fighting with their addiction. Please know that there is hope. There is always hope.

See yourself as pure and unadulterated. Hammer that image into your brain until it seeps down into your soul. Know that you are a God-made, God-purposed being here to do great and noble things.

Somewhere along the path, you believed the lie. You swallowed the pill that convinced you to settle for less. Afterall, everyone in your family is overweight and all your friends smoke! You stepped in your own way with some cockamamie story, and now it's time to step back out of the way.

Shifting your core belief will take your journey from one of struggle to one of honoring and loving yourself.

It's time to remember. It's time to hit refresh on your beliefs about yourself. And it's time to reintroduce yourself to the world from your fresh new perspective. The world has been waiting for you, my friend. Let's flip it!

16

CREATE YOUR
OWN LUCK

THE STORY WE TELL OURSELVES

Lady Luck will catch up to me some day. I'll just keep plugging away at what I'm doing and someday I'll get lucky.

FLIP IT **Make your own luck. No waiting, no wishing. Luck is when your preparation meets timing.**

> *"Twenty bucks says I don't*
> *have a gambling problem!"*
> *— Rob*

If you get busy doing your part only, then you can actually create your own luck!

On our spree through Vegas, Franca and I were like fish out of water. We stood there, staring at the gambling tables, not having a clue where to start. Throughout my years, I never picked up drag racing, puzzle building, or poker.

So, what do you do in Vegas when you don't have a ticket to a show, and you don't understand poker? You go play the one-armed bandit. Anybody can pull a lever, stand there and yell, "c'mon c'mon!"

I'm sure I don't need to tell you how the day ended. Of course, we exited the building with less cash than when we entered. But the thrill of anticipation sucked us in, hook, line, and sinker.

So, wouldn't it be great if you could unlock one of those machines and manually line up those cherries, three in a row? Or how about just two in a row? We have to keep some sort of sport in it. The good news is, you can do that with your life. You can line up the first two cherries, and then leave that third cherry to life.

HERE'S WHAT I FIGURE

In life, we're always up to something and hoping for the best. We're trying to get our kids through college or land that big client. We're trying to build that dream or buy-in at the right price. Or maybe we're trying to find that perfect mate and we just need a little luck on our side.

FINDING YOUR PERFECT PARTNER

So many things had to line up and take place for me to find my perfect partner. How could I possibly be at the right place at the right time to find her? I mean, it's a big world out there, and there are tons of fish in the sea! Here's how I did it; I simply lined up the first two cherries, and then I let the third cherry come find me when it was the right time.

What did those first two cherries look like? The first one was me spending time making myself into the man for whom my perfect partner was out there searching.

Making myself a more valuable commodity, so to speak, would certainly bring that first cherry in alignment. So, I became a student, learning more about love and life. I studied my past to prepare for my future. I

110

learned more about what that proverbial "Mr. Right" looks like. I made myself more "marketable."

My second cherry was all about getting myself squared away spiritually. If I wanted God to be the pillar in my relationship, then I needed to be spiritually OK with myself. I could then present myself as a "whole" rather than a "needy half." And so, I did.

The third cherry was not my concern. It will happen when it happens. Letting go of controlling that third cherry was key. Can you guess what eventually happened? My sweet 'n sassy Italian girl appeared on the scene. And I married her! Hi Franca!

Another example would be my career as a writer and speaker. Seems like everyone and their dog wants to write a book. For years, I had several books floating in my head, but they were all a dream with no legs. There was no intention or resolve. So those three cherries never lined up. My dream never fell in my lap with a cherry on top. (See what I did there?)

It took me making the choice to get up and move! Move my feet, move my intentions, move that writing pen. As I put my intentions into motion, opportunities began to show up in my path. When my dream became my divine obsession, I put myself out there to the world through clubs and groups. As I write this, I am literally still lining up those first two cherries, knowing that the third will eventually align. Hey, it looks like it already did. You are here reading my book! Yeehaw!

BOTTOM LINE ⌣

Take the bull by the horns and maneuver those first two cherries into place. Do the work. Hone your craft. Make your dream an obsession.

Polish yourself better than you've ever been before. Get clear and define what your first two cherries are, and then get busy.

Take a typing class, learn real estate, find and shadow a mentor, invest in online courses, meet new friends and spread the word, learn the Texas two-step, get your feet dirty, hone your skills and get better and better at what you want to be and do. Consistently improve yourself. Always be better today than you were yesterday.

BE a Proactive doer. In doing so, you're lining up those first two cherries and setting the table for the third. Then let go of what happens from thereon. The third cherry is out of your hands.

Learn the language of the champions. Eliminate from your vocabulary "I need to." That's the voice of your passive side, giving you the excuse to put it off another day.

Reminder

God might be waiting for you to do your part so He can do His

"I should" is another phrase you must throw overboard. That one keeps you comfortably parked in mediocre. Do not allow yourself the luxury of using "I should." My "I should's" are telling the world that at least I know what I need to do. But I'll be darned if I'm actually going to do it!

Replace "I need to find another job" with "I'm finding another job now." Remove "I need to do better with that," and replace it with, "I'm getting better with that." Oh, and "someday" never gets here, so do it now. Remember, the first two cherries come from your skill sets and your earnest efforts. They represent your asset or value that you bring to the table. And the third cherry? That's all of that talent and effort striking the right time and place for the big payoff!

You and I can't see when and where that right time and place will be, so don't allow it to consume even a smidgen or a smudge of your thoughts. It will happen when it happens, so let it go. It's called faith. Invite the miracle by thanking God in advance for the en route blessings.

This concept works for you in every crevice of your life, from finding employment, to making that sell, to finding your perfect mate.

Seneca, a Roman philosopher, once said, "Luck Is What Happens When Preparation Meets Opportunity." Well said, Seneca.

 Let's go with this one: Luck is what inevitably happens after you've lined up your first two cherries. God does His part after you've done yours.

You create your own destiny. As a man of faith, I believe that my God has a strong hand (the upper hand) in the matter, but He did attach legs to our frame for a good reason. So, let's take the hint!

In my experience, whenever I'm tending to those first two cherries of bettering myself, God always follows up with the icing on the cake. He's faithful in delivering that third cherry.

Reminder

LUCK is what happens when Preparation meets Opportunity

Seneca

The good news is, when you let go of the outcome, you then get to enjoy the freedom from worry and doubt. You'll then have the energy to pour your talents and efforts into the one thing you have power over: Yourself.

Stop wasting your time and energy waiting and wondering and worrying. Let go and live your life! Better yourself daily, laugh aloud in the process, and thank God for the blessings that are already on their way!

The Serenity Prayer:

God grant me the serenity to accept the things I cannot change, the courage to change the things I can, and the wisdom to know the difference.

The Cherry Prayer:

God grant me the peace to accept whatever the third column brings me, the courage to create the first two columns, and the wisdom to remember which column is mine and which column is yours.

17

YOUR WHY WILL
TELL YOU HOW

THE STORY WE TELL OURSELVES

Work harder, longer, and faster. Sacrifice is what it's all about. You'll succeed. And you might even get to see your family... someday.

FLIP IT **Your WHY is your power. It's your "pull." Without it, you'll have to muscle your way through. Good luck!**

> *"Do what you are called to do, and
> your work becomes play."*
> — Rob

There are two ways to get your wagon up the hill. Pull it or push it. But wait, what if there's a third way? What if you could sit inside the wagon while something else pulls you? Now we're talkin'!

Stephen Covey came up with the phrase, "Keep the end in mind." Bingo! That concept opened a whole new world for me.

In sales school, we learned all about the carrot and the stick. It's kind of a game you play to light a fire under your tail (the stick), and to give yourself a prize to chase after (the carrot). Companies have spent fortunes creating carrots for their salespeople. From European vacations, to prize money to a corner office with a window, it's all to provide the carrot.

On the other hand, the stick was there to scare you into performing well. Keeping your quotas up will keep away any penalties.

I was all in on the game. I even used it with my own employees. And yet, I always had the gut feeling there was a better way. And I found it. It's the Power of the Pull!

Here's What I Figure

One of my mentors, author and speaker Jim Rohn, once said, "Work hard at your job and you can make a living. Work hard on yourself and you can make a fortune." Thanks, Jim.

I WAS STUCK ON MY HOW

I had to figure out how I was going to make enough money to sustain us, or how I would make enough headway to meet my deadlines.

How will I expand my base? And how can I ever make a living with just this? How? My how's kept me thinking, doubting, analyzing, worrying, and most importantly, *not moving*. I was stuck on how.

Don't get me wrong, I'm a big fan of designing a good blueprint before starting anything. However, there comes a time when you have to act before you know all the answers.

My WHY for writing this book is what gives me the strength and fortitude to work endlessly, day and night, to perfect it and bring it to you.

Without my WHY, it would be a task. Have you noticed how many author-wannabes are running around out there?

It seems like everybody *wants* to write a book. I was one of them. And, like the rest of that club, I never put pen to paper, because I couldn't figure out how I could pull it off. How would I publish it? How would I sell it? I was stuck in how-gear.

I then came nose to nose with my burn, my passion, my WHY. And that's the love that I feel for you. Yes, you. I may not know your name, but you are my WHY. My desire for your best is the fuel that pulls me.

I have a relentless obsession to paint a picture for you that will give you the perspective that I'm now enjoying. I want you to have the freedom, joy, and fulfillment that comes from flipping your thinking! This is my contribution to your success in life. And at the same time, it feeds my sense of purpose.

"How" once kept me from taking leaps of faith in all areas of my life. I then got clear on my WHY, and my world changed.

YOUR WHY IS YOUR POWER

Stop waiting for your how's and get busy on your WHY. Your how's are God's domain. Your WHY is yours.

Be all about your WHY. That's your reason you are doing what you're doing. That's your power. If you feel no power, zip, or energy, then it's time to stop the show and get back to your WHY. We simply need to put that cart back there behind the horse.

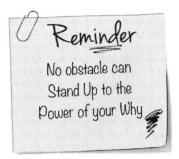

Reminder

No obstacle can Stand Up to the Power of your Why

Whether you are growing a marriage, building a business, parenting children, or attending school, you eventually come to a choice-point where you have to choose to let go. You have to release your white-knuckle grip on controlling the logistics and just fall into your WHY.

We want so badly to keep control and to feel confident that we know exactly how it's going to all work out. We want to feel safe. And that mind-set will keep you safely and soundly broke.

Obstacles are minimized as your WHY runs them over like a worn-down speed bump. No hurdle, block, or obstruction can stand against the powerful pull of your WHY.

Burnout, boredom, fatigue, and depression are signs that it's time to get clear on your WHY. When there's no WHY to pull you, then life is all about pushing, striving, struggling, and fighting...and burnout.

Without your WHY in clear view, you simply have to do your best to stay motivated and to keep battling until you hopefully get there.

"Y'all ask too many questions. Just keep pushing!"

Flipping your thinking from "how" to WHY takes you from motivated to inspired, from your brain to your heart, and from the push-push-push to surrendering to the pull.

A great moment in our history was when man discovered the power of the wind on maritime voyages. Before that time, tremendous manpower was necessary to muscle the oars and keep the boat cutting through the tide. Then some smart guy figured out how to lasso the power of the wind by using a sail. Genius! That breakthrough invention allowed ships to gracefully and effortlessly slice through the waters.

 Your WHY provides wind for your sail. It offers power for your journey, just like wind provided the power for the voyagers.

The logistics of your what's and how's can overwhelm you with data and deadlines and second-guessing, while your WHY keeps you grounded and connected to your source, as it steadfastly pulls you forward.

No doubt, it sometimes helps to light a fire under your own tail. But when that needed push becomes the norm, it's time to make some new choices (your tail can only stand so much fire before it's toast).

Your job or career must never become drudgery. Either change your work, change why you do your work, or change you. Life is too short. Trust in the process, trust your intentions, trust that God will honor, favor, and bless your efforts. Keep your purpose and your reason in front of you like a hockey puck, in every aspect of your day, and you'll seldom feel overworked.

Reminder

Work hard and you can make a living. Work hard on yourself and you can make a Future.   Jim Rohn

Do what you love or fall in love with what you do, then you'll never "work" another day in your life.

BOTTOM LINE

It's time! It's time to flip the very reason you get out of bed each morning. It's time to move beyond "just because."

So many are trapped in the repetitive abyss, simply going through life's motions. We've come by it honestly. We were told a long time ago that we have to go to school, get a job, get married and have kids. But WHY? Without your WHY, life becomes daily repetitive and predictable motions.

What's your reason? There's a reason you have a job. And if "to make money" is all you can come up with, then burnout will catch up with you sooner or later.

If your reason for being self-employed is just to make money, then let's go deeper.

What's your reason for doing anything in your life? If you want to catapult from boredom to fulfillment, you must take the time to define your WHY.

Here's your hint: Your most compelling WHY is in your contribution to the world. Contribution is what this life is all about. Figure out where it is that you are contributing, where you are making a difference, then sell out to that effort. Establish your WHY around it.

A school bus driver was bored with her assignment. She saw it as just a job. The mundane repetition was killing her until she got clear on how her job was making a difference in the lives of her kids. That's her WHY. That's power.

An accountant's job can be quite routine until he plugs into how he is helping each of his clients build their own dreams. When his day becomes about contribution to others, he then feels the power of the WHY.

> **Reminder**
>
> You are who you are because you have deemed yourself as "That's who I am."

Are you self-employed? Why? Get past the money and the fame. How specifically are you improving the lives of others? How are you making a difference?

Mike the "My Pillow guy" is making a killing! But he's doing it by helping us all be more successful after a good night's sleep.

Have you heard of Johnny the Bagger? If not, Google it. But first, grab your tissue; you'll be inspired. Yes, even a grocery bagger can have a powerful WHY.

Your WHY is your ticket. You were created with a purpose in mind. And when you fall into your WHY, you'll become invincible. And you'll watch your world around you transform, as things begin to work in your favor.

18

EXPECTATIONS
AND OTHER DELUSIONS

THE STORY WE TELL OURSELVES

Hey, I give 100 percent, and so I expect everyone else to give 100 percent. That's just how it should be. Everybody should pull their own weight, owning their stuff, doing their part, playing by the rules, and, by golly, just doing what's fundamentally right! No free rides here, mister.

FLIP IT Your expectations, though maybe justified, will keep you bunched, stressed, resisting, and disappointed.

"No matter how much I lower my expectations, some folks still manage to roll right under 'em!"
— Rob

Your expectations, as reasonable as they seem, are setting you up for upset, agitation, and disappointment.

Here's sobering truth that will rescue you from yourself: Your disappointment in people and in events isn't about them—it's about you.

Me personally? I come from the old school of expectations. I expect things from people, by golly.

"I expect them to act that way."

"I expect things to fall into place."

"I expect her to clean her room."

"I didn't expect him to react that way."

"I expected her to at least show some interest!"

"I expected them to say thank you."

"I expect him to not drive like a maniac!"

Is it confession time now? OK, I'll go first: I wrestle with expectations. I can muster up a brain-freeze from upset when I think that someone "should have or could have or would have." What's wrong with people!

I'm thrilled to share with you my exciting discoveries about expectations. I figure we need to have *some* expectations. I mean, how else can life work?

Can you relate to any of these?

- Ordering your overpriced steak medium rare for the second time, only to see it come back well-done...again.

- Nearly being run off the road by a teenager zooming past you, weaving dangerously through traffic.

◆ Saying hi with a smile to someone and getting a snarl in return.

◆ Giving your child the one simple task of taking out the trash, then coming home at day's end to find that he didn't... again.

◆ Meeting your friend for lunch and wasting thirty minutes of your precious time because they showed up thirty minutes late without calling.

◆ Sitting bumper to bumper for forty-five minutes, certainly was not on your schedule!

Expectations. They're a normal part of our everyday life, right? Shouldn't we have at least *some* expectations of people? Isn't there a minimal code of ethics written somewhere that tells me I should expect something from folks?

 At the restaurant of expectations, I was able to order a platter of disappointments, an entrée of frustration and anger, and for dessert, I got me a big ol' bowl of broken friendships. And the nice people there even gave me a coupon telling me that if I became their loyal customer, I would be guaranteed ulcers. What a deal!

Here's What I Figure

I can expect and expect and expect until the cows come home. And when the dust settles, folks are still going to do what they will do, regardless of my expectations. And so, the only person all in a tizzy is me!

Let's crank that expectation into a delicious alternative. Flipping your expectations into anticipation will bring you a much better deal.

The key difference? Expectations are born from fear, while anticipation is rooted in faith and hope. Every emotion, attitude, or mind-set that you and I have has an origin in either faith or fear.

My fear of something happening or not happening will stir a selfish, controlling agenda. That shows up as expectations, leading to frustration.

On the other hand, faith breeds acceptance, patience, and a willingness to let go.

I anticipate my Houston Rockets making the playoffs next NBA season. I certainly will not expect them to, but I'm hopeful. Have you ever seen an emotionally ravaged fan? That's what staunch expectations look like.

Your joy is never altered by circumstances in your world, but rather by how circumstances did not match up to your expectations.

It's not about what people did or said that upset you. It's about what they did or said that didn't align with your agenda.

Your attitude of expectation can project to the world a sense of entitlement: "It owes me this." The truth is, it owes you Nothing! Have you ever given a gift to a child who feels entitled, or maybe a dozen roses to a lady who just expected them? *<Insert deflating balloon sound here>*

When your recipient "expects" you to give him or her a gift, it takes the joy out of giving, and you don't feel appreciated.

Shakespeare said, "Expectations are the root of all heartaches."

When you expect, you "set in stone" your rules for a specific outcome. And, by golly, other people better shape up and cooperate with your plans!

126

While expectations come from a camp of fear (doubt), anticipation is born of faith (love). Anticipation is an inner giddiness that looks like hope and has no outcome chiseled in stone. Oh, it sees clearly what it wants, but it's not shackled to a specific destination.

Franca and I enjoy traveling by car. Those Boeing pilots never let us take a U-turn at peach stands or waterin' holes. So, automobile it is! Before we travel, we establish our destination and route. But we've learned that our trips never unfold according to our scheduled itinerary, so why invite frustration to join our trip?

Our destination is in stone, but our route is in pencil. With that mind-set, we're able to relax and enjoy the scenery without worry. That flexible approach allows us to truly enjoy the journey.

ANTICIPATION CARRIES A SENSE OF GRATITUDE

Franca takes care of many things around our home. I don't expect her to, but she does. And because I don't expect it, I appreciate each and every time she folds my clothes or dusts my office. I think of her actions not as her expected duties, but rather as her acts of love. And so, I express my appreciation to her.

Anticipation   ⟶   Feel appreciated   ⟶   Harmony & fulfillment

Expectation   ⟶   Feel taken for granted   ⟶   Resentment & isolation

When you feel appreciated, your entire perspective shifts. According to a recent study, one of the top reasons employees stay at their jobs is for feeling appreciated. Appreciation even beat out the paycheck. What does that tell you about how we humanoids are wired?

OH, BUT WHAT A PRIVILEGE TO HAVE TWO LEGS!

When was the last time you thanked God for your legs? I didn't for the first thirty years of my life. Why? Because I expected to have two legs, and so, I didn't think about it. Do you realize how many people worldwide don't have two legs? Have you ever stopped to envision what one hour of your day would be like if you didn't have two legs? I invite you to stop right now and do that. How fortunate you are to have both legs! And two eyes. And two ears. How blessed!

In so many ways, our expectations have lulled us into taking many gifts like that for granted.

Lord, I'm so grateful for these legs! I'm so very grateful.

Now, after feeling that pure sense of gratitude, and after clearly envisioning what life would be like without your legs, tell me how you

Reminder

When you stop expecting perfection from folks, you can finally like them for who they are

feel about yourself and about life. If you truly stopped and felt these words of gratitude, you were probably moved in some way. You may even have a little condensation in your eyes. Don't worry, my lips are sealed.

That, my friend, is gratitude. Now, carry that sense of appreciation for every tiny piece of your life that, until now, you've simply expected to have.

Flip your thinking! Rather than expecting the sun to rise, thank God for another spectacular sunrise! Rather than expecting to see colors, break out of the lull! Marvel at the miracle of contrasts and shades and depths of field!

Rather than just eating as usual, stop and take in the vibrant colors of your foods. Thank God that they are not gray tasteless mush. What a variety of colors and textures and flavors were given to you and me! Holy cow, such a creative, inventive, ingenious Creator we have! What a magnificent experience, this experience of life! Somebody pinch me!

BOTTOM LINE ⌣

Ding ding ding! Here's your wake-up call. Let's sharpen your sense of appreciation. You'll do this when you start heaving some of those expectations overboard. I want to start hearing some splashes.

Turn down the volume of your expectations of people and things. Position yourself to enjoy them for who and what they are, rather than for what you think they should be, or for what they can do for you.

I want you to experience a sense of fulfillment, both when life goes your way as well as when it appears otherwise. FLIP IT!

I want to speak directly to you "Expecters" out there. (Yes, it's a word. And don't bother looking it up. I just invented it.) All you staunch Expecters are assuming that things and people should line up correctly.

Expecting things and people to line up with your plans works well in military drills and safety inspections, but it doesn't work in matters of life and love. I'm sure you've seen enough proof of this by now!

Hold on to your plans and dreams. Expect the best from yourself. It's extremely important for you to have a clear vision of what you want, of where you're headed, and of what you're willing to sacrifice to get there.

It's equally important to remember who's God and who's not. Carry out your plans with humble anticipation, enthusiasm, and a sense of appreciation for every twist and turn, because they are all here on purpose. Flip your interpretation of those twists and turns. They are here to help shape and hone and protect and guide you.

I thank God for my broken road that led me here to you. Yes, to you.

19

WHAT YOU HAVE
TO HAVE YOU'LL
NEVER HAVE

THE STORY WE TELL OURSELVES

I HAVE to have that! I cannot be truly happy until I catch that man or have that ranch or reach my goal!

FLIP IT **Let's find your joy internally, then you'll stop pushing away the things you want in your life.**

*"Happiness abounds when you let go of
the thing you thought you needed
to be happy."*
— Rob

Whatever in this world I require for my happiness, I will somehow push away for fear of not having it.

Three years after their wedding day, Tom and Cindy agreed that it was time to start a family. But they had difficulty conceiving a child. The following three years of fertility programs and alternative attempts left them exhausted and disappointed. Oh, and childless. They forfeited their dream of having their own child.

And, of course, you can probably guess what happened next. Two months later Cindy conceived! But it was after they let go and surrendered their need to have that child.

I counseled a couple, Dan and Sandy. They had tied themselves in knots trying to make their floundering relationship work. Sometimes struggling efforts can keep you from the very things you want. I asked Dan if he was willing to give his bride permission to leave him. He answered, "Are you crazy?"

Reminder

Whatever you feel you MUST have, you'll never have.

I wanted to bring them both to the place of surrender. Their stress level was silently killing the relationship. Somehow, I eventually helped them release the white-knuckled grip they both had on their union.

Their fear of the relationship falling apart was setting it up to do just that: fall apart.

Fortunately, we eventually got there, and they were both able to relax and let go. And letting go paved the way for love to eventually resurface. Today, their family and home are restored.

What, in your life, do you feel compelled to possess for your happiness? A husband? A wife? Kids? More money? Bigger house? Faster car? Successful business? More friends? Nose job? Butt lift?

If I believe that I MUST have a woman in my life to be happy, then what do you reckon will happen if I get lucky enough and have one? I'm going to do whatever I must to keep her from leaving!

She *must* stay because I cannot lose my happiness! And so, I quietly gather all my needed arsenal. Anything goes here because she simply cannot leave. Now, I may need to do a little lying, manipulating, and sacrificing my own wants or needs. I might even have to adjust my values, just to keep her happy.

Oh my, sounds very unappealing, doesn't it, ladies? But you see, I simply *must* have her! I cannot let her go, because then she will take my happiness with her.

From the get-go, I am actually functioning from the fear of losing her. Jealousy and doubt may eventually consume my thoughts, as my conversations become less genuine and less present. And before you know it, all my fears become a self-fulfilling prophesy.

Here's What I Figure

I'm a big fan of hard work and going after what you want in life. The abundant life is yours! Go get 'em, tiger! But yet, there's an invisible obstacle, a fear-based mind-set that keeps you shooting yourself in the foot.

It's one thing to go after what you want from a position of love (faith), and it's an entirely different animal to chase what you want from the fear of not having.

There's a beautiful hymn with lyrics that I want you to carry inside you. **"It is well with my soul."** When all is well with your soul, there's no more fight or struggle for what you want. And in that state of mind, your efforts will attract the things that you want, by virtue of who you are.

HAVE WHAT YOU WANT

Having the life that you want starts with being OK with the life you already have. I'm not implying to

settle for what you have, but rather to feel contentment. You will no longer function from frustration or from lacking. Your demeanor will calmly and steadfastly move toward the life you desire.

For all you partner-seekers out there, let's try a new dance. Stop spending your efforts looking for that just-right partner and start carving yourself into that just-right partner. FLIP IT! Do your part, then watch God do His.

Remember, you are constantly transmitting energy into your world. Are you sending "I'm needy" or "I'm content?" Are folks sensing from you, "I'm looking for happiness," or, "I am happy?" One energy repels, the other attracts.

YOU ARE ENOUGH

Sit right here and let's get to the heart of the matter. You are already enough, my friend, just the way you are. And you'll continue to grow and learn and progress.

You were made in God's image, and He's quite fond of you. Don't ever lose that perspective. You are crafted from love, with everything you need already factory installed. Know that, honor that, and be that.

Reminder

Having what you want starts with not needing it

BOTTOM LINE

Fall in love with yourself and with who and where you are in life. Joy isn't over there, it's right here, right now. And your belief that your joy and success in life is "out there" will keep you on a futile wild-goose chase.

Here's my promise to you: As you become OK with where and who you are in your life, and as you fall in love with your God-made adorable self, you'll notice a shift inside and out. Your efforts and actions will come more from contentment, rather than from fear. And that will show up as less struggle.

Ironically, you'll have more of those things you desire when you let go of your requirement to have them.

PART THREE

FLIP YOUR CHOICES

20

HAPPINESS IS
A CHOICE

THE STORY WE TELL OURSELVES

Someday I'm going to be the happiest ever! That's when I'll finally have that new boat, big house, and the love of my life.

FLIP IT **When the dust settles, your happiness will simply be a choice that you'll make to be happy.**

*"Money can't buy you happiness, but it sure
puts a good down payment on it."*
— Rob

After you've exhausted ways to find, buy, or build your happiness, you'll eventually discover that it was a mere choice all along.

Someday I'll be happy. Oh boy, I can't wait for that day to arrive!

When I get my new car, then I'll be so happy.

When I finally retire from this rat race, then I'll be happy.

If we can just get our kids outta the nest and off to college, we can finally be happy.

Meeting Mr. or Ms. Right? That's when I'll find happiness!

So much of our joy is contingent on external props lining up just right.

Now and then, we hear the shocking news that another rich celebrity committed suicide. But they seemed so happy! I was personally stunned by Robin William's choice to take his own life. Here was a man who made a living making folks laugh, yet in the end, his suicide suggested that perhaps he couldn't find his own laughter.

Reminder

Some wait for sunny skies while others carry their own weather with them

Happiness seems like such a slippery commodity!

The ancient Greeks said, "Happiness is the joy that we feel when we're striving after our potential."

Aristotle said that happiness is a state of activity.

The all-wise Siri claims that it's "the state of being happy." Hmm, sounds like Siri might make a great politician.

Our pursuit of happiness takes up a lot of time! Every choice we make is directly or indirectly linked to bringing happiness, even those tough choices that may not feel happy at the time.

The lie tells us that our joy is somehow attached to our new car or that island vacation or our partner or our dog. But, as you and I have witnessed, such joy is conditional and temporal. Don't buy the lie. "Out there" only triggers the joy that is already inside you.

I did find joy in my marriage and in my first car and my first house. And my first pickup truck put me up there with George Straight and the rest of the gang. I also noticed that it wasn't enough. Those "things" were somewhat cyclical, and sometimes unstable or conditional. And so, I kept having to invent new things to do or buy so I could hit "refresh" on my happiness.

What is this evasive hockey puck we call happiness? And, where can I find it? Is it something I hunt for, or is it something I earn? Or maybe some of us are simply hard-wired for happiness and others are not? And isn't my joy at least partially related to my environment?

Here's What I Figure

Everybody is different. Wherever I find joy might be different than where you find it. I have noticed that folks tend to find their happiness in at least one of these four sources:

Happiness from PERFORMANCE

These are the conquerors of the world. Climbing Mount Everest brings fulfillment to the climber. And there was surely a deep sense of achievement when Bill built Microsoft and Steve built Apple. But then what? What's next?

The performer's trial is found in the down-turn. What goes up must come down. Life's ebbs and flows keep the mountain climber perpetually searching for that next high, no pun intended.

Happiness from STARDOM

Remember Freddie Prinze? He was young, handsome, funny, and seemingly loved by everyone. Freddie took his own life at a very young age, at the peak of his success. And so did many other stars who seemed to have everything one would need for happiness!

What happened? Once they reached stardom, the happiness they sought wasn't there. I hate when that pot of gold isn't at the end of the rainbow!

Happiness from BAR-LOWERING

If I lower my expectations of myself, I won't fail. Genius! My life will then be a success by virtue of no defeat. I'll just snuggle up in my cozy, comfy, mediocre existence, along with my carefully selected mediocre friends. We will all have a beer on Friday night and talk about everything under the sun *except* those dastardly dreams that we never really had a shot at anyway.

Happiness from THINGS AND PEOPLE

I think we've all experienced happiness through vacations, new toys, a big house, money, good friends, and a loving partner. And, we've also experienced grief and unhappiness when they rust, fade, die, change, or disappoint.

What about you? Are you happy, truly happy? And if so, how did you get there? Where did you find happiness? If you're not sure, then it's a good idea to figure it out so you can be assured of keeping it.

HAPPINESS IS A CHOICE

I lost my good buddy Rich not long ago. Miss you, Rich. He was one of my favorite phone calls to make, because he frequently reminded me that happiness is a choice. I remember Rich pontificating, "That's what separates us humans from animals. We can make the choice to be happy."

"But how can I be happy when my client dumps me or my money runs out"? Simple answer: Choose to be happy.

 The difficulty is in the deprogramming. You've adopted the lie that there's really a connection between external stimulus and your internal joy. And that fallacy keeps you climbing the ladder leaned against the wrong tree.

CHASING ONE'S TAIL

Wayne Dyer told the cat story. It's a great reminder of what happiness is. He talked about an old alley cat that noticed a kitten chasing its tail around in circles. The old cat snickered as he watched awhile.

He finally asked the kitten what he was doing, and the kitten answered that he learned in school today that happiness was found in his tail. And so if he could catch his tail, he would then have eternal happiness!

Slightly amused, the old alley cat told the kitten that, being out on the streets for thirteen years, he learned the same thing the kitten learned at that Cat Philosophy School.

The kitten excitedly asked him if he caught his tail and found eternal happiness. The old cat said, "No."

The kitten stopped and asked what happened. The wise old alley cat assured the kitten that, indeed, happiness is the most important thing to a cat. And it's true that happiness is located in the tail. But he found that if he goes about his life, living the way he wants, his tail follows him wherever he goes.

There's a saying hanging at the entrance to my hallway: "Life isn't about waiting for the storm to pass; it's about learning to dance in the rain."

You'll experience happiness when you stop pursuing it.

"What did he just say?"

Your happiness is not something you hunt, chase after, or strive for. It's something you choose. Do yourself and the world around you a big favor: choose happiness. It looks so much better on you than that other fabricated stuff!

HAPPINESS IS A THOUGHT

You become what you think about. If you sow unhappy thoughts, then you'll reap unhappiness. It's that simple. Give it a whirl: Try thinking about one of your happiest moments in life and at the same time try being unhappy.

Happiness is a state of mind that you choose in this very moment.

I know, I know, I can hear some of you now, "It's not that easy!" Well, now, hold your horses. I said nothing about it being easy. I said it's simple. The choice itself is simple. Where the difficulty comes in is the process of dismantling all those definitions, wrong meanings, and mental habits you've built around the word happiness.

Claiming your joy is often nothing more than "un-
doing" old stinkin' thinkin'.

One of God's greatest gifts to us is the freedom of choice.

He permits us to make our own way in life, and to forge our own paths. For that I am grateful. Some folks complain, "Why did God allow that to happen?" Because bad choices go with the territory of freedom of choice. Otherwise, it wouldn't be "free choice." But it beats the alternative of captivity in Puppetville, wouldn't you agree?

THEY TOOK MY STUFF!

I remember returning home one day and finding my residence pillaged. My home-sweet-home was absolutely ransacked. I mean to tell you, all my "stuff" that once felt so cozy and safe was now either broken or stolen.

I remember walking in the door, looking around and being overcome with that strong sense of feeling violated. I quickly pulled myself together and thought, "I have two choices on my plate. Bitter or better." I could choose anger and resentment, or I could take a deep breath and come to grips with what just happened.

Feeling violated and shocked, I chose the latter. It wasn't so much a choice of right or wrong but a choice to be happy vs. unhappy. This life ain't no dress rehearsal, my friend, and you and I don't have time to spend it being angry.

I could have held a resentment, and it could have eventually festered into a get-even rage. And a large part of me wanted to go there.

 Remember, your choice to resist what happened is only your futile attempt to change the past.

I allowed myself to feel the initial anger. I deserved it. But I did not let those scalawags steal my joy. This was a huge breakthrough for me. Everything that happens in your life presents to you a gift, my friend. For me, this gift was my chance to step up to the plate and take a swing at the curve ball that life just tossed at me.

I hit it outta the park. I didn't crumble to the bad guys. I did not strike out. I held my integrity. "Smack!" That was the sound of me giving myself a high-five.

Reminder

You are not a product of your environment, but your environment is a product of you

It's justifiably easy for you and me to stake a claim to our anger. "They had no right to do that," or, "He can't cut me off like that!" Or, "They fired me for no reason! Now how am I going to pay my bills?"

And what about those bigger challenges? You know, when your best friend dies, or the doctor remorsefully tells you that you have one month to live? Those are bigger life-choices, yet the same simple decision awaits you: Happiness, yes or no?

"But there are so many other variables involved! It's more complicated than that!"

Yes, there are other variables involved. And I do not intend to discount your pain. That pain is your right. And...you also deserve joy. A victim of physical or emotional abuse can certainly attest to the pain. And, as complicated as the chattering of your mind might make it seem, it still boils down to one simple choice. And choosing happiness certainly gives you resourceful power and grace to work through the pain.

HAPPY TOOLS

One tool is a question I ask myself that always helps me keep a healthy perspective is, "How is this thought going to serve me?"

That's it! Your thoughts are powerful. I want you to take one thought at a time and consider its value. Just one thought can lead you to either happiness or sorrow.

Here's another favorite tool to put in your tool belt. Proverbs 2:11 reminds you to LET UNDERSTANDING GUARD YOUR HEART. This has helped carry me over the mountain a few times. You can't mix oil and water, and you can't mix empathy and anger. Let understanding guard your heart as it helps keep you from judgment and rage.

Choose to understand, rather than to clam up and judge. Judging is the easy choice. Empathy takes courage and humility while keeping your heart and mind open to life.

After seeing my home pillaged, the easy choice would have been to carry hatred in my heart. And I actually did for a while. Was I justified in doing so? Was I right? "Wrong and right" serve us in basketball fouls or traffic tickets, but not in life. Justified or not, you choose happiness or hatred. I've been justified and miserable before. Have you? That particular day, I chose happiness over hatred, and it served me well.

HAPPINESS IS BEING IN MOTION

You're like a bicycle in motion, built to move. If you stand still, you'll fall over.

If you're at a standstill with your career, your marriage, your direction, or in your spiritual life, then your remedy is simple. No thinking required, and it's available this instant with free delivery. Hey, that's better than Amazon Prime! You simply need to move. What kind of movement? Well, I'm glad you asked.

Start with the simple. Make a difference in someone's life. Trim your neighbor's hedges, watch their kids while they go on a date. Cook a meal for someone. Serve another in some capacity, and then tell me if that doesn't start you on a better path. And while you're at it, rearrange all your living room furniture.

Dr. William Ishak, a professor of psychiatry at Cedars-Sinai, says studies have also linked random acts of kindness to releasing dopamine, a chemical messenger in the brain that can give us a feeling of euphoria. This feel-good brain chemical is credited with causing what's known as a "helper's high."

Reminder
Joy is found in the gettin' there, not in the arrival

Get involved. Join a breakfast club or charity or cause. Grow. Learn. Progress. Move. Read. You'll then experience a new sense of fulfillment and happiness. Sounds simple? It is. Life's answers are always found when you get back to the basics.

 Such an ironic critter, this state of happiness. You get it not by trying to get it, but by giving it away.

Walt Disney died before Disney World was ever built. He only saw it built in his mind. He had the dream and the passion, and he moved toward that dream. He never saw his vision come to fruition, but I feel certain that his joy was found in moving toward his dream, every eye-twinkling moment of it.

I just heard someone object, "But I stay busy and I'm still not happy!"

OK, let me talk with you Project Addicts out there. We need to put some purpose into your motion. Let's flip that busy-ness into contribution to others. Start making a difference instead of just making time. Join a small group at your church. Clean out a friend's closet. Pay your neighbor's water bill. Start a charity. Go beyond just staying busy. Advance yourself and others!

THE TWO WOLVES

An old Cherokee Chief was teaching his grandson about life. "A fight is going on inside me," he said to the boy. "It is a terrible fight, and it is between two wolves. One is evil. He is anger, envy, sorrow, regret, greed, arrogance, self-pity, guilt, resentment, inferiority, lies, false pride, superiority, and ego."

The Chief continued, "The other is good. He is joy, peace, love, hope, serenity, humility, kindness, benevolence, empathy, generosity, truth, compassion, and faith. The same fight is going on inside you, and inside every other person as well."

The grandson thought about it, then asked his grandfather, "Which wolf will win?"

The old Cherokee replied, "The one you feed."

Bottom Line

No longer allow yourself to buy into the non-truths and lies. This will take some practice. You've got to shed yourself of that victim's mind-set that wants you to focus on anger, blame, worry, and disorientation. You're bigger than that.

Happiness is not a feeling, emotion, or product. It's a choice. Your choice. So, choose it.

Happiness is a result of your choice after choice to be happy. Feed your wolf of faith, while starving your wolf of fear. Toss some meat to your wolf of patience and understanding and humility and starve your wolf of backbiting judgments and egotistical conclusions. And in doing so, you'll stay equipped to deal with the predicament at hand. You will function from a place of joy, rather than from a place of despair. The choice is a no-brainer!

Your happiness is a valuable asset that no one has the power to steal. No one.

21

CONTROLLING LIFE

The Story We Tell Ourselves

I must control how I look, what people think of me, and what will happen to me tomorrow. If I don't take charge and micromanage my life, I won't succeed.

Flip It Your attempts to keep control over your life are keeping your life out of control.

"You know you've arrived when you can finally stop controlling people and things. You know, the ones that you never really had control over anyway."
— Rob

Your effort to control your world is a battle you'll never win. Ironically, letting go will bring you more control.

Have you stopped to consider how much time you spend during the course of an average day trying to either gain control or keep it?

We try controlling our children, our temper, our spending, our budget, our diet, our emotions, our job security. We also try controlling our appearance, our health and fitness, our home security, our dog, and even our future.

We just love feeling in control. I know I do. It gives me a sense of assurance that everything is in its place and I won't encounter any bad surprise. Ah, feeling in control sure is comforting.

I once planned an outdoor picnic for three hundred people in my side yard. I felt in total control with every detail down to the number of pork ribs. Then it rained. It wasn't supposed to rain. Suddenly, I felt a strong sense of just how *not* in control I am.

In our relationships, we like those guarantees. You're going to stick with me, right? You're not going anywhere? Perhaps that's why we "go steady" and why we sign a marriage contract. "Finally, I caught her. Now I can relax and get about my life because I'm guaranteed she'll be here tomorrow." Well, we all know how volatile those marriage contracts can be.

Controlling your kids? Don't get me started.

Controlling my business or my job? As an employee, you want to be assured that you'll have a job tomorrow. And as an employer, you do what you must to still be in business tomorrow.

You pay your employees just enough to keep them coming back while keeping your prices low enough to keep your customers coming back. It's a game of controlling things and people.

Reminder

You'll lose control when you try and control

From the cookie jar to Treasury securities and mutual funds, we learn the art of controlling our money. Or, at least, *trying*.

Whew! Controlling life is a fulltime job! My life reminds me of a great big chessboard. And my chess pieces are my kids, my work, my friends, my dogs, my challenges, my emotions, my money, my thoughts, and my events. I'm constantly shuffling them back and forth on my chessboard, trying to predict, forecast, anticipate, and manipulate!

WE ARE ALL CONTROLLERS

You may be thinking, "I'm not a controller." That's only because you've gotten so good at it that you're even fooling yourself. We all try to fashion our environment. The in-your-face overt controllers are easy to spot. They are the micromanagers, keeping their thumbs atop everything and everyone in sight.

Those fellas just haven't yet learned the art of stealth- manipulation. My mama used to joke with us, "I let your father *think* that he's in charge."

The craftier controllers are the passive-aggressive ones. They hate confrontations, so they'll just hone the art of deflecting, blaming, undermining, and ignoring. But it's all-controlling, by simply trying to further our own agenda.

Ben is a friend of mine who wanted a partner so badly that he kept pushing away his chances. He engaged with online dating for awhile, but he never made it past the first date with any of his "candidates."

Reminder

Whatever I grab eludes me and what I release wants to stick around

It all changed for him when he understood this control concept. He was sure of what he wanted: he wanted a life partner. That was his goal and so, by golly, he had his target in place! Every glance Ben cast was calculating and assessing and weighing, "Is she the one?" Now, how do you reckon that mind-set showed up in small talk with any of his "victims?"

Your intentions always reveal themselves, no matter how tricky your ploy might seem. Our intentions show up in our mere inflections and posture and eye movements and suggestive remarks.

My friend Ben frequented a dance hall here in Texas. But boot-scootin' was the last thing on his mind. He was all about the hunt. I asked him once during lunch what was the first thing he did when entering the dance hall. He replied, "I canvas the place, mapping out where the babes are." His radar was up, and the hunt was on!

There's certainly nothing wrong with wanting to find a partner. But when you project your have-to-have like a skunk projecting his spray, prepare yourself for rejection. Remember, you're always coming from either love or from the fear of not having.

In trying to maneuver any outcome, I'm functioning from the presumption or fear that it's not going to maneuver by itself. It needs me to make sure it happens, or else it won't happen. That's when I become the clog in the flow of life.

Hunting works well for fish, deer, and Texas wild hogs, but it doesn't work with people and with matters of love and life. Nobody likes to be caught, sold, or bamboozled, am I right?

Years ago, I tried saving my sinking marriage by urging her to talk. She wasn't one to express easily. Have you ever tried making someone talk? I think that one is right up there on the difficulty chart next to trying to nail Jell-O to a tree.

My wanting her to talk seemed like a reasonable desire at the moment. I mean, talking is important in a relationship, and I knew that ours was starving for it. But, from her perspective, my desire probably felt like pressure. And with time, I'm sure it began to feel demanding. In hindsight, it's clear that my "insistence" brought me the opposite of what I wanted.

Here's What I Figure

It's all about delivery, and you can't fake delivery. You're either coming from love or from fear, and the person opposite from you knows it and feels it, no matter how much sugarcoating you apply.

The harder you try to control, the more out of control and unmanageable your life becomes. It's a law.

Remember that life around you and the people in it are not "things." They are living energy. They are God-crafted souls, just like you, and they have their own purpose and path. You are in their world, just as much as they are in yours.

You cannot control or contain energy any more than you can squeeze water in your hand. And your fear that you cannot control it will only push control further away.

YOU'LL GAIN CONTROL WHEN YOU RELEASE CONTROL

As an employer, I learned to back off from my need to micromanage (control). And, by the way, you micromanagers are not as in control as you might think. You'll soon learn the difference between cooperation and temporary tolerance from your people.

My efforts to control my employees always bred mistrust, resistance, an unfulfilling work environment, and a lack of loyalty. Letting go of control brought me results that were, at times, undesirable. But it eventually groomed trust, fulfillment, and a sense of appreciation and respect, both to and from my employees.

We've heard the stories such as the child growing up and leaving his or her strict home, only to go berserk the minute their feet hit the ground of independence. The parents may have thought they were in control through those growing years, but the truth always rises to the top, like cream in a milk can.

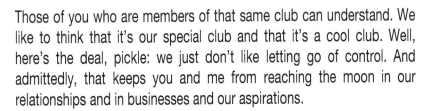

You may be thinking, "But I have a hard time letting go."

I can relate. I'm a do-it-yourselfer. Letting go and delegating are two painfully difficult tasks for me.

Those of you who are members of that same club can understand. We like to think that it's our special club and that it's a cool club. Well, here's the deal, pickle: we just don't like letting go of control. And admittedly, that keeps you and me from reaching the moon in our relationships and in businesses and our aspirations.

Controlling might serve us in building stuff in our garage or cleaning out the attic, but it's not serving us in life. So, how about we just disband that club? Are you with me?

 I had a bad dream recently. I thought it was real, and when I awakened, I was so relieved! The same holds true with control. You may think you're in control, but you'll eventually find that it was just an illusion. Your picnic will get rained out sooner or later.

Life is always reminding you of just how not-in-control you really are.

Here's how you gain more manageability and control in your life: Take your faith in God and in people and lift it from a noun to a verb. How? By practicing trust. Practice delegating. But remember, whenever you delegate, you must let go. C'mon, you can do this!

HEY PARENTS!

My most challenging moments of parenting were my struggles to keep from controlling my kids. I mean, the world is tough out there, full of drugs, scalawags, and bad guys. Everything in me wanted to protect them from those early days, but I knew better. I knew then that I could not possibly control their thoughts and actions. I could only equip them with the tools they needed to make wise choices, and then let them go. That took faith.

Some of you may be thinking, "I wish I knew of this when my children were younger." When you're past the formative years, it's an entirely different ballgame. But there's hope! And I invite you to connect with me and let's talk about it.

HEY, YOU BOSSES AND MICROMANAGERS!

You'll witness the joys that Scrooge himself experienced, as your expectation/appreciation scale tips. Practice expecting less and appreciating more. That's when your company will begin operating as a real company rather than an autocracy. People will give you their gut-effort when they feel your appreciation.

YOUR FRIENDSHIPS WILL FLOURISH!

Be careful. Because, as you let go of controlling life around you, you'll see a shift in your friendships. People will actually like you! Puff on that one awhile! But here's your warning: You may have to buy a bigger house to accommodate your expanding Christmas party list.

Folks will respond to you differently as you control less and care more. Your self-serving agendas will take on the face of true friendship and you'll attract folks like white on rice. (Or as we say down here in the South, like flies on a cow patty.)

Loosening your grip will actually bring about more of those changes you tried getting back when you were busy trying to manipulate them into existence. Yeah, those.

To be sure, you'll still be scheming your plans and honing your skills and attacking your dreams. But you'll not be weighed down by your required outcomes that kept you fighting life's flow.

OK, brace yourself. This one might make all you controllers get up to go spike your coffee. When you surrender your need to know exactly how things and people will turn out or perform, and when you get out of your own way, you'll then set the stage for Miracles! OK, I said it. I went there. *Miracles.* Now, we controllers don't like that word, because we can't figure out how to manufacture it, regulate it, manipulate it, bottle it or even explain it. But, wow, letting go of my "have to know how" gets me out of life's way.

When I release my need to know exactly how money will show up, or how she will react, or how I'm going to pull this one off, or how the end will turn out, I'm clearing the path for life's natural process. My manipulative approach is no longer mucking things up, and thereby miracles are free to dance!

God is doing us a favor around every corner, and sometimes we notice it. For that controlling side of you, God patiently sends opportunities to practice letting go. Have you noticed, or are you too busy controlling?

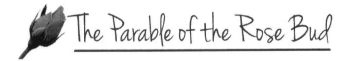

The Parable of the Rose Bud

What do you do when you receive a rose that's not yet opened? Do you stick your thumbs in the center and start prying it open? Of course not! The bud will die if you do, and you'll have nothing but petals on the floor.

So, of course, you'll do your part for the rosebud. You'll give it water in a nice vase, maybe add a little plant food, and perhaps a bit of Mozart playing in the background? You'll do what you need to do to support its natural growth. So, tell me, why do you keep trying to pry open your relationships? Your efforts to control the pace and direction of any relationship, from friendship to partnership, are like prying that rosebud open for your own selfish timetable. That's not your job.

Your job is to grin 'n feed it what it needs. Period. Get straight on what's your job, and what's God's job. Then stand back and let life deliver to you the miracle of the rose.

BOTTOM LINE ⌣⌣

Everyone and everything has been placed in your life by no accident or mistake. They are each a vital part of your classroom, assembled just for you to practice letting go. They're not here for you to control, they're here for you to learn how to let go of control. How are you doing so far?

Here's a great mantra for you seasoned and accomplished controllers out there. Tattoo this on your thinker: "GOD'S GOT THIS."

How does that feel? How does the notion of stepping out of the way and letting go of your desired outcome feel? A bit uncomfortable, like a wedgie?

Reminder

When I stop trying to control, I can enjoy those things I could never enjoy while trying to control

Continue doing your part. Put in the work and press forward while letting go of the rest. Release your need for everything having to "look" the way you insist it should look. And for Pete's sake loosen your grip on those how's. And while you're at it, practice applauding and celebrating the actions of others, rather than scowling under your breath, "I would have done it differently."

Go ahead and feel that urge inside you to take charge. Recognize it. Give it a name. Then practice stepping out of the way and letting people make their own blunders. Life wants to flow on its own path, not yours. I'm telling you this because I love you! I want you to experience the beauty and the marvel of being the vessel and not the clog!

Flip your controlling urges into desires to serve and support and learn and expand yourself. You'll then watch life unfold for you in ways you can't even imagine inside that little controller-brain of yours.

Let go and let's go!

22

GOOD NEWS FOR
PEACEKEEPERS

THE STORY WE TELL OURSELVES

Confrontation is bad. And so, life flows much smoother by just doing whatever I must to keep everyone happy.

FLIP IT **Your efforts to calm the waters are only ignoring the boat that keeps causing the ripples. Fixing is temporary, healing is divinely permanent.**

"A new brake pedal doesn't make
your car stop better."
— Rob

Life is showing you where the fracture is, but you keep covering it with a bandage.

There was once a king who was stuck by a thorn. He hated that thorn because every time he bumped against something or someone, it hurt! And it only pushed the thorn further into his arm.

He covered it with a large pad. That didn't really solve the problem because, now and then, he would forget that the thorn was in his arm and... Bump! Ouch!

He then had his servants design a sort of insulated padding to wrap around his entire arm. Surely that would do the trick.

After a few trials and errors, he finally got it right. But it was a bulky, hideous contraption that kept him from participating in all the games and social activities he loved. But at least the thorn in his arm wasn't agitated.

We are that prince. We carry around with us internal irritations and aggravations from long ago. Maybe our thorn is an unresolved marriage issue or a traumatic childhood experience. You know, the one that keeps rearing its ugly head in your adult relationships? Or, that belief that you're not good enough, smart enough, pretty enough, lovable enough, or successful enough. That's your thorn, that's the part of you that you're protecting with choices that only keep you from fully enjoying life.

You have been protecting yourself from feeling pain whenever someone plucks that string or bumps against that thorn because it hurts! And it only reminds you that, on some level, you're not enough.

Your efforts to cover them up and protect yourself from the pain has become your conditioned salve. After all, who wants to feel pain? But those walls that you erected, while protecting you from pain, are also isolating you from the world around you.

We live in a world of quick fixes. We don't want to be bothered, because we just don't have time. So, will somebody please just patch me up and get me on my way? I have a schedule to maintain, and I would really rather not be bothered with this.

Mandy was a feisty independent farm girl in South Dakota. She had no siblings and was raised by two working parents. They rarely had time to spend with their daughter. When Mandy was seven, her father abandoned the family. As a small child with a blank life-canvas to paint, Mandy painted an image of herself not worth sticking around for. After all, if she wasn't good enough for her own dad, surely another man would see no value in her as well.

She wasn't consciously aware of this self-belief, but it was alive and well and keeping her from enjoying normal relationships. She built "emotional contraptions" around herself so that her partner would never know her on an intimate level. Her thorn was well insulated. She feared if a man ever got to know the real Mandy, then, like her father, he would abandon her.

Mandy's "fix" was to avoid any resemblance of depth in her relationships. The fix never healed the wound; it only kept her padded and not feeling the sting of unlovable. It also kept her from the normal activities of a healthy union.

We've become quite skillful at building contraptions around our thorns. Those contraptions come in different colors and shapes. We get very crafty, from defensiveness to shyness. Your "contraption" might also look like drinking, smoking, overscheduling, perpetual projects, avoiding topics, parties, or people. This is to name only a few.

These methods do a bang-up job of keeping you from having to face the pain and discomfort of what you fear is the truth about yourself. You'll do anything to keep someone or something from irritating that thorn!

Here's What I Figure

I once had dry skin on my feet. Franca told me to listen to my body. "Your dry skin is telling you something."

I didn't understand it at the time. I mean, if I have dry skin, shouldn't I apply moisturizer? That seemed like common sense to me, but not to Franca.

Did you know that your dry skin might possibly be your liver speaking the only language it knows? Who woulda thunk! My liver had been talking to me, trying to get my attention through my dry skin. And here I was, muffling its voice with skin lotion.

We are inundated with a market trying to sell us bandages to cover up compound fractures. Figuratively speaking, of course. Listen to your body. Pay attention to what it's telling you. And listen to your emotions. Be proactive in looking for solutions that are root-correcting, rather than symptom-appeasing.

If you can't sleep, the answer does not come in pill form. If you're depressed, the answer is not served by the glass. Your answer is always within. Go within or you'll go without.

Bottom Line

Become a good listener to the world around you. So, you lost your job...again? So, your relationship ended...again? So, your child got into trouble...again? Repeats are tugging at you, my friend.

Practice the art of listening.

If your car wheels squeak, stop squirting WD-40 on your tires. Consider what's causing the squeak.

162

Stop ignoring, fighting, or medicating the messenger and start hearing the message. That third time you were laid off or fired from your job is a signal! It's time to be still and listen. Consider what the common theme is: it's you! You can only blame others for so long before you go batty. Take notes and own your part. Listening and gathering good information can show you the way to bigger and better things.

So, you just broke up with another guy... again? Stop. Flip it! This time, go for the cure, not the fix. The temporary fix is in finding another guy; the cure is in finding another you. Be still and shift your thoughts away from him and what he did wrong. Shift your focus onto yourself, and what part you played in the matter.

 Stop trying to find better, and start *being* better.

Listen to what your world around you is trying to tell you about yourself. Perhaps you've been blinding yourself to that great big pointer that's revealing how you keep setting yourself up for failure or for disconnect or for disappointment. What are you doing to keep intimacy at arm's distance, or to keep real connection away? How are you literally keeping opportunities from crossing your path and finding you?

I want you to do this because I want you to have the love and the life that you deserve, as well as the treasures that your God had in mind for you, back when He took you out of the oven. You'll have it when you choose to get better. And life keeps bringing to you opportunity after opportunity to do so.

Remember, your answer is never "out there."
That's only the fix. Go for the cure, baby!

So, your child got himself in trouble...again? When will you finally stop and listen? God is patient and loving, sending you valuable messages through the people and things in your world.

Maybe the solution doesn't lie completely with your child. Could your parenting skills possibly need tweaking? Could this be about scolding them less and loving them more?

FLIP IT. Stop greasing the noise and start healing the cause. See every problem as a flailing flag, trying to get your attention. Your angry partner is only expressing their pain from within. Stop attacking their ungraceful antics and start raising your awareness and curiosity to understand what's at the root of those antics.

See their pain, not their behavior. Take your eyes off the swinging arms and see the bruised heart within.

We're all a bunch of hurting children trying to find our way. So, clothe yourself with empathy and understanding. See your own need to heal, as well as recognizing that same need in others. Listen to your body's cry and answer its call. Those temporary fixes only keep you from living the full life for which you were designed.

23

RE-ACTING

THE STORY WE TELL OURSELVES

Wow, did I just say that? Oh boy, that's going to get me in a heap of trouble. But hey, my reaction was justified. They caused it.

FLIP IT When you flip your reacting into responding, you'll see more possibilities as you do less discarding and more engaging.

> *"How people treat you is their karma;*
> *how you react is yours."*
> — Wayne Dyer

Today you will be given countless invitations to either:

1. React (counter against)

2. Respond (engage with)

Picture this: You've pulled the freshly roasted turkey from the oven and set it on the serving table. The second you turn your back the dog jumps up and grabs the turkey and dashes out the back door. Holy cow, the dog grabbed the turkey! So, what will your reaction be?

As for me, once my heartbeat subsides back to humanness, I would probably have to contain myself from grabbing my shotgun. I picture myself scolding the dog, and then throwing him in timeout. And then, later, I would regret it. "Why did I scold the dog? After all, he was just being a dog."

Today you will encounter information from all sides. A problem, a circumstance, a criticism, a thought. You'll be given the choice to either react or respond.

Here's What I Figure

I've watched and noticed that my reacting usually takes me in circles. Sure, anger and upset can be somewhat appeasing in the moment. But like that big chocolate candy bar at the checkout counter, it really doesn't do me much good in the long run.

Today you'll have plenty of moments to react or to respond. Notice how you are constantly shaping your world, largely by how you react.

Reacting to criticism only keeps you from seeing benefit or value in what was being said or done. Reacting to folks who disagreed with you only keeps you from considering other perspectives. Reacting to your friends or your partner only pounds a wedge between you while keeping you from truly engaging.

Reminder

You cannot control what happens to you but you have total command over your response

Reacting to that negative bank balance only keeps you shaking and wavering and unable to confidently confront and fix the root issue.

Emotional reactions never truly serve us; they keep us isolated from people and from acknowledging whatever internal issue is being triggered.

 Whenever you react, you are literally "re-acting" out some part of your past. There's a stored memory being triggered. And you are merely knee-jerk reacting to the finger that pulled your trigger. Like Pavlov's dog, you are "salivating" or reacting to some past incident or experience.

The technical terminology for this phenomenon? "Wow, he really knows how to push my button!" You're welcome.

If your daddy made you shut up at the dinner table back in the day, then your adult-self might react to criticism by retreating. If you felt falsely accused as a child, you may be overly defensive as an adult. If you were emotionally or physically abused in a relationship, then intimacy is something you may avoid. If your past partner cheated on you, then you might have a short fuse with jealousy or mistrust.

**Whenever your old wounds are exposed,
you'll have an internal urge to re-act.**

We each carry with us our unresolved past experiences and our own programmed reactions. Those reactions rear their heads now and then, but all for good reason. The antidote is not to push them down or to drown them out, but rather to heal their "thorn."

We sometimes choose to put a silencer on those triggers. We justify that some subjects are taboo and better left alone.

Clearly, you and I are designed to grow. Have you noticed that growth typically follows some sort of discomfort or pain? Your learned reaction is a skill that you perfected to protect yourself from emotional discomfort. And yet that emotional discomfort is the very passageway to healing and growth. This is Huge! You've seen this play out in something as innocent as inappropriate laughter.

Have you noticed that life is constantly nudging you toward resolving, healing, and breaking free? Thank you, life!

You might receive professional advice to set your boundaries and not allow things and people to penetrate you. While boundaries can certainly be a healthy choice, just be certain those boundaries you set are self-loving, not self-isolating. Your world around you is filled with messengers, teachers, and nudgers trying their best to get your attention and help you heal and progress.

You were created for greatness. I want you to master the art of gracefully responding to the world around you.

Come here and let's throw some pebbles into that crick over there. I want to share with you a secret.

Manipulating and boundary-setting can give you some space to help you reset, catch your breath, and gather your thoughts. But don't be afraid to eventually face that fiddler. The fiddler isn't as scary as you have concocted in your mind.

Bottom Line ‿‿

Join me as a fascinated student of life. Fascination beats frustration any day of the week.

The next time you feel yourself starting to react, try pausing. It's OK, the world will wait for you. Now, count to ten. Then make the conscious choice to respond rather than react. What's the difference?

Being responsible is choosing to avoid autopilot reacting. Make a more conscious choice. Think of the word responsible as "able to respond." Responding looks like engaging rather than resisting.

I know, I know...your button is pushed. Stop criticizing the button pusher and this time, look within. Recognize what it is inside you that's flaring up. What is trying to get your attention?

Remember, you only have two choices: Either wake up (learn to respond) or keep sleeping (react again). One is doing life "on purpose," and the other is ignoring the issue and reacting like a pinball machine.

Responding keeps you on the path of growth. Reacting keeps you stuck in a repetitive abyss, only to repeat the same negative experience in the coming days.

Reruns? No thanks! That's for Friday night TV and pizza with my honey and my two mutts.

EXIT THE TREADMILL!

Whenever you catch yourself upset at someone or something, your choice to respond will allow you the opportunity to step off the treadmill. You'll take your focus off them and what they said or did, and you'll look directly at your own upset. C'mon now, you can only shoot so many messengers in your lifetime. Isn't it much simpler and more serving to just read the message?

Consider how reacting to people and things has been stiff-arming you from dealing with life. Adopt a new meaning to that outdated childhood lie that you've carried in your backpack all these years. You're an adult now, and it's time to reframe and redefine, baby!

You might be thinking, "But he needs to change! And she needs to stop that!"

Perhaps they do. But no matter how thin you slice anything, there are always two sides. There's a growth opportunity for them as well as for you. And guess which one you need not concern yourself with, and which one is yours to own?

Your choice to react will bring you an entirely different experience than your choice to respond:

⚡ Reacting **separates** while responding engages.

⚡ Reacting **judges** while responding considers.

⚡ Reacting is **emotional**, responding is logical.

⚡ Reacting is **instant**, responding can be delayed.

⚡ Reacting **closes doors,** responding stays available.

⚡ Reacting makes a **mess**, responding makes amends.

⚡ Reacting **resists**, responding resolves.

⚡ Reacting **kills** relationships, responding heals them.

⚡ Reacting **undermines**, responding understands.

⚡ Reacting **defends**, responding defers.

⚡ Reacting brings **regrets**, responding invites healing and renewal.

Become a student of yourself. Pay attention to how you react to your environment. Learn new healthy habits of responding to life, especially when life doesn't cooperate with you.

Reminder

Being responsible
is being able to
respond

Remember, reacting will keep you resisting and closed, as well as plum worn out. But responding will keep you open to new possibilities, while it energizes you and helps you further define your journey.

Let's do an immediate flip on this one. Start now. React less and respond more. Take those baby steps; pause and recognize when and where you react. Practice being responsible by responding!

24

DO MORE
BY DOING LESS

THE STORY WE TELL OURSELVES

If you're not staying busy, and if you're not doing something productive with your time, then you are not making progress. You won't be profitable, effective, and successful if you don't put it in gear.

FLIP IT **Don't just do something; sit there!**

"Life. It's the thing that passed you by back when you were so busy doing."
— Rob

You can get more done when your plan of attack starts with being still and present.

What? What did he just say?

Abraham Lincoln once said, "Give me six hours to chop down a tree and I will spend the first four sharpening the ax." Being still helps you sharpen your ax. It refreshes, recharges, regroups, and redefines your very reasons for running the race.

My childhood days were spent playing in the hot 'n humid Houston climate. Our air-conditioning system was a few noisy window units mounted in the most important rooms of the house.

There was no better feeling than coming indoors from a hot and sweaty afternoon, splashing water on my face, and standing inches away from that A/C vent. Whoa, that cold air billowing from that rickety Frigidaire window unit was always the recharge I needed to get back out there for another session of kickball.

During the brutal months of July and August, we stayed inside more than outside. Whenever our TV-watching time crossed the limit, in came Mom with her announcement:

"Kids! Don't just sit there...DO something"!

You probably heard the same command during your kid-years. And so, we all developed this "stay busy" mentality. I never quite became a "project maniac," but I did find myself staying busy just to stay busy.

HERE'S WHAT I FIGURE

Some of my most production insights have come from my still-times. When we're still, we can then hear beyond the overpowering noise of the world.

It takes an effort to be still, as oxymoronic as that sounds. Today's technology keeps screaming at us so you'll have to make a few decisions, such as turning off that TV for the moment. Oh, and, you'll need to...brace yourself for this one...put your cell phone on silence. You heard me. Honor your much-needed still time by eliminating all distractions.

Reminder

We are human beings
not human doings

174

Life works on all cylinders when you're in sync with yourself. Whenever your actions line up with your thoughts and your values, then life hums. To be fair, it's easy to forget what it is that we do value because we all get so caught up in life's noise!

Not only will you gain more clarity with your thoughts, but you'll make a huge contribution to your health. We all know the toll that stress takes on our heart, blood pressure, weight gain, weight loss, and so much more.

My mom's voice echoed in my head through the years, reminding me to "get busy." She meant well back then, and truthfully, it kept me from becoming a lazy bump on a log.

Psalm 46:10 tells us to "Be still and know that I am God."

You might be thinking, "But I don't have time to be still."

The truth is, you make time for everything that matters most to you. So, the root problem here is that you haven't yet convinced yourself that it's important to be still.

 Your choices to be still keep you living from the inside out.

BE STILL

Take charge over your volume control and frequency. Ironically, being still is one of the most productive activities you will choose during your day. Noise tends to force its way into every empty space you'll allow, leaving you spiritually, mentally, and emotionally exhausted.

Sometimes I'll lay awake at night, unable to fall asleep. I can't seem to slow my mind as it races through my day. And we've all tried making ourselves not think thoughts. How ridiculous is that, trying not to think? It only leads to more thinking!

So, those sleepless moments present the perfect chance to practice being still. Thank God for your health, for your home, for your friends. Thank Him for this masterpiece called life. Thank Him for your breath, for your eyes and ears.

Thank Him for His love and grace.

When I take my mind to the land of pure gratitude, I'm sometimes awarded the most peaceful refreshing night's sleep.

I invite you to FLIP how you hold this thing we call prayer. Consider it as simply "being still with God." Here's what I discovered when it became less about "asking for favors" and more about being in His presence. As I lowered the volume of my own mind's jibber-jabber, and as I quit trying to "get things" from God, I began to hear His voice.

Being still in prayer began to look more like thanking and praising and appreciating and marveling. And I began losing "defined time slots" for prayer as it transformed to a 24/7 connection.

Mother Teresa suggested that "we need to find God, and He cannot be found in noise and restlessness. God is the friend of silence. See how nature—trees, flowers, grass—grows in silence; see the stars, the moon, and the sun, how they move in silence. We need silence to be able to touch souls."

THE BIGGEST THIEF

You and I rob ourselves from being still with the chatters of our minds. It's hard to turn off your self-talk. Not only is the majority of your self-talk negative, it's also typically about yesterday or tomorrow. Seldom is your self-talk about the here and now.

Bottom Line ⌣

Incorporate into your day a moment of being still. It's not going to find you, so you will have to consciously find it. In my world, I position myself alone and still with my coffee and my two worthless dogs and my journal at the start of each day. I start by emptying my mind. This may take some practice. Your quiet time might be on the drive into work without the radio, or at night in the silence in your bedroom.

There's no right or wrong answer; the important thing is that you start.

Yesterday is history, tomorrow is a mystery, but this moment is a gift. You reckon that's why they call it the present?

Practice being in the present. When you eat, pay attention to the flavors and textures. Appreciate the experience. When you go outside, get in the habit of looking up and acknowledging the artwork we call sky. Stop. Listen. Hear. Count how many things you are sensing in this very moment, from sounds to sensations.

 Learn the art of being still. It's in that space you'll begin to lower life's noise-volume and hear the music. That music will give you new perspectives and creative insights. That's where you'll hear your own inner voice, your dreams, your soul. It's there where you'll hear the voice of your Maker. And that, my friend, is where you'll find many of the answers you're seeking.

25

MAKE YOUR MOVE!

THE STORY WE TELL OURSELVES

It's best to wait until everything is aligned just right before I move. Timing is everything. So let's wait. And wait. Even though I have a great idea, let's just wait until the wind is blowing westward and the temperature is more comfortable. And even then, we may need to put more thought into it and wait.

FLIP IT MOVE, ALREADY! Bringing home the bacon requires one frequently forgotten ingredient: LEGS.

> *"Talk is cheap because supply exceeds demand."*
> *— Rev. Bob White*

There comes a time when you must transfer movement from your lips to your legs.

I know what you're thinking. "This guy just talked about being still. Now he's telling me to get busy"? OK, so it appears I'm off my rocker. Stay with me.

I love sitting with a good friend and a brewski, talking about life. It's safe. It's cozy. I don't have to move while I'm sitting. When I sit and think of ideas, I'm a monster! I'm an invincible king! I'm an unstoppable entrepreneur in my own mind! But when it comes to putting them into motion, gosh...it's time to go grab another beer.

This world is filled with great thinkers with no legs.

One of my focus groups was called "Bean Soup." We met twice monthly to visit and share meaningful life topics. The topic during this particular night was "Moving vs. Thinking."

We were all seated in a big circle as I asked them to look around the room and tell me how many doors they saw. I told them that I could see three from my seat.

I then stood up and walked about ten steps to my left. From that perspective, I spotted five doors. I was able to add the back door and the closet door to my list because of my new angle.

I could have sat and thought and thought and thought. I could have looked harder and looked harder again. But I would still have only seen three doors. It took getting up off my tush and moving so I could see more doorways.

At twenty-one, I started my first business. A California company wanted me to manage and eventually own their Houston franchise, and so I did.

I was a master at drawing up plans and creating incentive sheets for myself and for my managers. I could use those color markers like nobody's business! I was great at "thinking." Oh my, what a great thinker I was! I sat back at the end of the day and thought, what beautiful graphs and charts! I should frame them.

My attention to creating pretty graphs kept me at a snail's pace. I was a great thinker. Hindsight is oh so clear, and I must confess to you here and now: I was chicken! Yep, I was a right-brained-thinking artistic chicken.

Whenever you and I overanalyze something, we catch the Paralysis of Analysis. And oh boy, does that ever keep us hogtied to the starting gate! We love to use that convenient excuse, "I need to give it more thought." That way, I don't have to move. And if I don't move, then I will never fail. I'm a genius!

Did you know that Michael Jordan missed 100 percent of the shots he didn't take?

I was one of those aspiring writers who claimed, "I'm going to write a book someday." I even came up with eight different book titles. They were great! They were genius! They were...nothing. They were nothing because they had no legs. And a legless intention is only a wish. I had a bunch of lifeless, legless wishes that looked great on paper.

I was a statistic. I was one of those dime-a-dozen geniuses in the world who had brilliant ideas but lacked the guts to claim my resolve and take the leap.

Here's What I Figure

When you and I move, other things move in response. Your movement gives you a different slant on things. When you move toward your vision, life miraculously meets you halfway. In my world, I notice that God moves when I move. My action draws His favor.

I had it backward! I was waiting for the world to move so I could move. But in truth, the world was waiting on me.

If you are without a job, Move! Get UP or shut up. Transfer all that energy from your mouth to your feet. Join a club, volunteer for a charity, meet new friends. Don't worry about "how" they might help you. Just Move! Trust me, your movement will shake things up.

Sitting at home will only keep showing you the same closed doors.

Reminder

It's better to try and fail than to never have tried at all

If you are lonely, get UP. Move! Stop thinking about it and join a club. Volunteer for charity.

If you are demotivated, Get UP. Move! OK, do you get the idea?

Here's the deal, pickle. You and I want guarantees. We want to be assured that we won't get hurt, embarrassed, tricked, inconvenienced, misled, or bamboozled. We don't want to fail, lose money, look stupid, or have regrets.

We love to feel in control of our destiny, and our behavior shows it. Can you relate to any of these?

- I can't ask her to dance; she might say no. And that'll hurt! So, I won't ask. Then I won't have to hear "no."

- I can't start my own business. I didn't go to school for that, and so I will probably fail. I'll just sit over here and talk about it and dream about it. I surely can't fail at that!

- I can't give my all to that relationship. What if it doesn't work out, and then I'm left with a broken heart? I just don't trust it. I'll play it safe and hold back.

- I can't take that leap of faith! I don't see how it can possibly work out! If I can't see it, then I won't buy into it. Better safe than sorry.

In thinking mode, we at least get to enjoy the fantasy of the idea, while avoiding any pain or gray hairs from possible failure.

FAITH, THE MISSING PIECE

That first step of faith is quite a remarkable experience itself. Stepping forward against all reasoning will set you up for seeing more doors! Your new perspective will expand your vision and shift your view. And you will stimulate your own ideas, as well as kindle other things around you. The pot will be stirred.

Even as I write this book, I have zero, zilch, nada idea of how it will be published, or even how it will be received. But, by golly, I'm writing it. I'm walking in faith. I'm confident the staircase will appear before me as I start stepping. And I'm believing that my heartfelt love for you, and my intentions behind my words, will fall on favored soil. In my mind, this book is already a bestseller.

> Reminder
> Feet in Motion set
> Miracles in Motion

Movement is the yeast to the bread. Are you ready for what I'm about to tell you? OK, buckle up.

MOVEMENT STIRS MIRACLES

"What? Did he just use the M-word"?

My dad told me to never pray sitting down. I now know what he meant. Your prayers alone, as well as your thoughts alone, are only half the recipe. That's like asking God to have the fish jump into your boat. You must cast your bait! Stirring action into the recipe is the yeast that will make it rise. Your movement will provide the catalyst that will bring it all together and make your dreams a reality!

Let's think this thing through. Think about where you are right now, and then where you want to be. You may be thinking about your primary relationship or your career. You may be thinking about your business or about your life course. Whatever it is, bring it to the table for this moment.

OK, let's get clear on this: You cannot and will not see the entire staircase before you take that step. You cannot know what his reaction will be, or what the market is going to do. You do not know how they will receive you. You cannot know exactly where your step will take you. That's why they call it faith. Living life full-out takes faith. And faith takes guts.

BOTTOM LINE ᗐ

It's time to FLIP IT. Put on those big boy britches and do faith for real. Your talk of faith is only as good as the action behind it. Proof's in the puddin', so let's make some puddin'!

 James Allen said, "For true success, ask yourself these four questions: Why? Why not? Why not me? Why not now?"

I used to pray, "God bring me stuff." Now, my prayers sound more like, "Lord, I'm walking. And I'm all ears and eyes; so point my toes in the right direction."

Reminder
Leap! When you do, the net will appear

When you move, things around you respond and start moving. If you're in a rut, step out of the rut. If you're in a repetitive hell, step off the merry-go-round. If you feel stuck, recognize how you, yes you, are keeping yourself on the treadmill, and act in opposition to it. Now, I don't want to hear, "it's hard!" I know it's hard. So just do it.

When you stop thinking and dwelling on the outcome (God's part) and you get about the business of action (your part), then great things happen.

This excites me to no end! It's OK to be afraid. Your fear serves a purpose. It spawns adrenaline. Feel the fear and move anyway! Exhilaration beats regrets any day of the week, so buckle your seat belt and step!

The difference between wishful thinking and dreams-come-true is simply your choice to **start moving**.

HOW TO CHANGE YOUR
HUSBAND

THE STORY WE TELL OURSELVES

If you don't like 'em, change 'em! Take the bull by the horns and make things or people into what you want.

FLIP IT Bringing about change in the people and things in your world starts with accepting them for exactly who and what they are. Quite ironic!

"Life runs smoother when you choose to accept an apology you never got."
— Anonymous

A hundred times today, you'll either accept or resist. And in the state of acceptance, you'll find the power to attract change.

My daughter went through a short-lived Gothic phase during her teen years. Her black wardrobes and a snug necklace that resembled a spiky dog collar made my daddy-alarm sound. She wasn't extreme, but I saw it coming. And every pore on my skin wanted to resist it. I'm glad I chose a wiser route.

As a parent, I was at a fork in the road. I could either stand up against her with my almighty dad-power, or I could try something different that did not include resisting.

The years have taught me that there is always a non-resistive way to deal with everything, including parenting. And because I took that approach, Jess was able to listen, and I was able to hear her as well. My efforts to understand her must have felt like acceptance (love). And in turn, she eventually made healthy changes.

Rather than words of shaming, I used inquisitive words to understand her. In place of threats, I used questions and common sense. Rather than, "You'll attract the bad boys," I let her find her own way with, "Tell me what kind of boys you want to attract in your life?" I helped her discover that this phase might not bring her what she truly wants.

To be sure, there are times to be the stern parent. But always coming from love. You want to be effective, not damaging.

Most importantly, Jess knew that I was coming from a place of wanting to help her, not to control her. It turned out to be a "black" phase. And let me tell you, that girl looks great in colors!

FAREWELL TO MY BRO

I lost my big brother and closest friend, Chris, at the young age of forty. His motorboat crashed, robbing us all of his vibrant life.

I felt as though a piece of me died that day. My brother and I were supposed to grow old together, and I had so many plans stored in my head. There were just too many memories yet to create with him. We were supposed to puff on cigars and sip brandy through many more seasons. I felt cheated.

I faced an excruciating choice, plain and simple. I could either harbor anger or accept the truth and make peace with it. This was the classic choice of getting bitter or better. How in Sam Hill do you make peace with losing your brother? I certainly had the right to be angry. And you certainly have a right to be angry at the guy who just fired you, or the market that just tricked you, or the girl who just dumped you, or the jerk who abused you. You certainly have the right to hate the jaybird who broke into your home, or the one who broke your heart. That's your right. And you can fight and resist all you want.

Thank you, God, for giving us the freedom of choice. I still miss my brother today, two decades after his sudden death. And I still wonder, "What if..." But I also recognize the futility in resisting his death. It is what it is. Regardless of how I feel about it. It's not mine to change, it's mine to find peace within it.

You know what takes guts? Acceptance. It's a conscious and counterintuitive choice that bucks every piece of your ego. I could have taken the easier road by telling my daughter to go take off those ridiculous black clothes. I could have grounded her or restricted her as a form of establishing my authority. Perhaps she would have changed. Perhaps she would have rebelled. But I saw that she was going through a phase that was very real to her. And that's key: giving others the right to their own experiences.

She, like myself and everyone else on this planet, was only trying to find her way. So, I practiced acceptance as I embraced her for exactly who and where she was in her life. And that bought me the ticket to connect with her, which set the stage for lasting, healthy change in my baby girl.

When I don't give something the full right to live, breathe, and exist exactly as it is, I then poise myself against it.

I married Jess and Alex's mom, knowing she was diagnosed with clinical depression. I fooled myself into thinking that I had accepted her condition. But clearly, I carried an agenda to fix her. I anticipated and even expected her to get better. Our intimacy suffered because of my expectations.

Hard lesson learned: Accepting someone means letting go of your plans for their life.

Your efforts to bring about change in anyone or anything comes either from your *selfish* desires (change for your sake) or from your *selfless* desires (change for their sake). And your true intentions are exposed to the world the second you realize that they ain't gonna change! Selfish intentions react with anger, upset, and resistance while *selfless* intentions may respond with disappointment, but also with love and patience.

Here's What I Figure

Full acceptance looks like wanting his or her best with no change required.

Period.

OK, this is where the power ignites, so buckle up. Love brings change, but resistance only accelerates the thing you're resisting. Did you get that?

Reminder

Acceptance is agreeing to live life on its terms, not yours

To be sure, there is nothing passive about acceptance. It actually takes guts to accept. It takes strength, as I must forfeit my own will for theirs. I'm called to put a leash on my ego and my agenda. Humility takes strength. Yet such strength moves mountains.

When I choose to accept and allow things and people to be exactly what and who they are, I have then positioned myself to influence change. Not only have I kept the door open between parties, but I've kept divisive resistance out of the equation.

A SEAT BELT STORY

I come from the old school of "no seat belts required." That's right, once upon a time, I didn't wear my seat belt. Then a new law passed requiring them. "Excuse me"? Oh, I wasn't rolling over on that one. Wearing a seat belt should be a choice of mine, not of the government.

Then years later, Franca enters my life from stage right. She's my feisty ball-of-fire Italian Godsend. No doubt, she was sent to knock some sense into me on many levels. Franca has many gifts, and one of my favorites is her gift of love-in-action.

So, no thank you. I didn't wear my seat belt for years. And yes, I heard about it for years from my kiddos. "Dad! Wear your seat belt"! It seemed the more they nagged, the more I resisted wearing my seat belt. I was like a big kid!

Reminder

The first base to bringing real change is accepting the thing you want to change

So, there I was, for the very first time, riding in my truck with Franca at my side. "I notice that you don't wear your seat belt." I fired back with a grin, "Yep." I was armed and ready, locked 'n loaded! I figured my quick "Yep" would snuff that deal, and she would know who's king in this truck. And it worked. That is, for that one ride.

The next time she rode in my truck, I came nose to nose with a superpower beyond my ability to contest. I was facing the power of a dainty loving woman on a mission.

How unfair! How unjust! The tables were turned, and I was now hopeless and helpless against this monster sitting right next to me!

She didn't fuss. Nor did she lecture or warn me. She didn't shame me or try to coax me into wearing my seat belt.

She didn't nag me or ignore me. Oh no, it was far, far worse than all of those! She brought out the cannon of cannons. She brought with her the one thing this egotistic cowboy just could not combat. She brought Love. And let me tell you, mister, that was like bringing a machete to a butter-knife fight!

Franca leaned over toward me, looked me square in the eyes with that sweet smile and charmingly claimed, "You look so very handsome wearing this seat belt!" As she said it, I heard a "click." All in one swooping motion, that woman had me buckled in, and I had no defense! I didn't know what hit me. I was helpless! What was a guy to do?

Fast-forward through a few months of, "You-look-so- handsome-when-you..." I now wear my seat belt.

It's just what I do! It's a habit. I never felt a fight or opposition from her. Without a resisting bone in her body, she changed me.

Your choice to accept will put you in a powerful position to create change.

When I accept you for who you are, rather than bogging us both down with my burdensome criticism or judgment, I'm then able to engage with you effectively, kindly, and constructively. To accept you is to love you, and love is the most powerful force known to man.

FIGHTING WHAT IS

When you and I fight what "is," then we are holding hostage all that energy and creativity that we desperately need so we can create the changes we want.

But they just charged me $100 for insufficient funds in my bank! I can literally feel my eyes constricting. My muscles are tightening as rational thoughts exit my body. My energy is vehemently sucked dry as I limp along on two cylinders.

Reminder
The Best Cure for
Anger & Upset
is Acceptance

Imagine that! Sapped energy and I'm not even doing anything! Except, of course, waging this inner battle against reality. That inner battle is pure thought, from the shoulda's and coulda's of my imagination.

The self-shaming, the feeling helpless and victimized. How depleting! Argh! Why can't I at least get a few calories burned from all that emotional activity?

Acceptance is typically the forgotten stepchild of any recovery or challenge. We typically zoom right past it, into fixing, panicking, resisting, denying, and judging. What a game-changer, to look at your situation squarely in the eyes and say, "Oh...you exist...OK...I get that. Now, let's deal with you."

 WHAT ACCEPTANCE IS NOT: Acceptance does not mean approval, consent, endorsement, condoning, or agreeing with. Heck, I don't even have to like it to accept it!

WHAT ACCEPTANCE IS: I resolved that, it is what it is, and that's what it is. That's acceptance. And until you accept it or them or yourself, you will always be second-guessing, debating, doubting, and showing one hundred shades of prejudice or bias. Acceptance is giving it your permission to happen or exist, and then we work from there.

BOTTOM LINE ⌣

Think of someone in your life who just ties you all in knots; the one that bothers the heck out of you. Now, take a deep breath and then I want you to accept them for exactly who they are. Yep, accept them.

C'mon, we have to practice this.

They are who they are, so let them be that. I want you to stop your judgment of what you think they should be, and acknowledge that they are purely, 100 percent who they are. And that's just who they are. Now, I'm not asking you to like them, I am asking you to let go of your complaint that they be someone they're not.

Reminder

Complete acceptance ends all drama

If you truly did that, then you would have noticed a shift in your demeanor. You became a tad calmer toward them. You know why?

Because calm isn't something you get by trying to be calm. Rather, calm is what's left in the absence of resistance. And when you and I let go of our fight, then we naturally coast toward peace.

For those of you still fighting, you go ahead and keep standing on your claim that the world should be different than what it is. And while you're at it, go ahead and hold a cement block two feet above your big toe and then drop it. Then claim out loud that gravity doesn't exist. It does, regardless of how you feel about it, or how opposed you may be to it.

Acceptance is a simple choice. If you can slow down long enough to see that your experience of life and everything in it comes down to making one simple choice after another, then you're on your way to mastering this amazing journey of life. I believe that the mother of choices you and I make in life is this choice of acceptance.

Let go! Let go of life having to stay in line with your plans and preferences. Give everything and everyone on this great planet the right to have their own existence, path, and lessons. They do, anyway, with or without you. And so when you step aside and let others have their own ride, you'll be able to

Reminder

Acceptance requires you to surrender your need to change your past

enjoy the ride of your life. And the cherry on top will be all that healthy change you'll bring about from your accepting spirit.

Yeehaw!

27

JUDGMENT, BRICKS, AND OTHER HEAVY STUFF

THE STORY WE TELL OURSELVES

Well, I'm not really judging, I'm just telling you my opinion. Besides, you really do look hideous in those pants!

FLIP IT **Judging others shrinks your world and stunts your growth. Oh, and it doesn't look pretty on you, either. There's a better way! Flip it!**

"Before you criticize a man, walk a mile in his shoes. That way you'll be a mile away, and you'll have his shoes."
— Steve Martin

Calling something or someone good or bad, or right or wrong, keeps you hogtied to misconceptions, while blinded from the truth.

We all tend to see the world in terms of good and bad, right or wrong, what's normal and what's inappropriate. We love to gossip about what's socially acceptable and what's bizarre. Judging others has become one of our favorite national pastimes. They even accommodate us in the grocery checkout lanes with tabloid magazines. That's so we can brush up on our judging skills while waiting to pay.

My intent here is not to dilly-dally with the psychology babble behind *why* we judge. Let's cut to the chase. Let's cover what matters most and how you can flip it.

In his book *Wake-Up Calls*, Eric Allenbaugh describes an episode from centuries ago when a farmer discovered that his prize horse had run away after breaking through a broken fence.

Reminder

Judgment closes doors while curiosity opens them

Eric describes how the farmer's neighbor saw what happened and commented, "It's too bad that your prize horse ran away." The farmer looked at him and replied, "Too bad? How do I know it's a bad thing?"

Later, to everyone's surprise, the horse returned, followed by a dozen of the finest wild horses that ever roamed the plains. They all ran right into the corral. The neighbor passed by and joyfully told the farmer how fortunate he was. The farmer replied, "Good fortune? How do I know it's good fortune?"

Later that evening the farmer's adult son attempted to ride one of the horses bareback and was bucked to the ground, breaking his leg. Hearing of the news, the neighbor grumbled how terrible it was that his son broke his leg. And, of course, the farmer questioned if it really was terrible.

It wasn't a week later when a ruthless warlord stormed through the hillside recruiting every able-bodied young man to fight his nearby battle. The warlord passed up the son with the broken leg. As of course the neighbor was delighted with the good news. And the tale continues.

Judgments aren't always negative, but they are typically premature. And those premature assessments can take us to undesirable places.

To the woman who was married twice to unfaithful husbands, no man is to be trusted. And so, she will keep any chance of intimacy at arm's distance.

The geek who never had a date in high school sees the opposite gender as unapproachable or intimidating. And so, he never gives himself a chance with girls. Our experiences form our bias, and our bias forms our judgments of folks. And, consequently, that judgment determines our quality of interaction with them.

JUDGMENT DIVIDES AND ALIENATES

When I judge you as being wrong, I then, in essence, close the door to any truly objective and open discussion with you. My judging you as stupid or crazy might inhibit or stop any authentic dialogue.

Judgment kills curiosity. Thanks, Thomas Edison, for not judging and labeling your first or twentieth or eightieth attempts to invent the light bulb as being failures! Otherwise, we might have all been sitting here in the dark!

Judgment is the easy way out. It's far easier for me to slap my verdict on something, rather than to be curious about its value.

"I judge my failed business as a bad business idea." Yes! Now I'm free from having to take any responsibility for my personal part. I don't have to learn or grow or take risks. I hate those risks, anyway. They're just so darn...risky!

"I judge my partner as wrong on that one." Perfect! I love being right. And she's wrong, so there's no need to explore why she believes or feels that way. And I don't have to consider an alternative to my view. Besides, we're fine just the way we are so why rock the boat?

"I judge him as arrogant." BAM! Bring that gavel down on that guy. I just won't bother connecting with him or knowing the real him. He's not my style anyway.

Judgment limits connection and expansion. Every time you judge, you hammer yet another nail in the coffin of growth and opportunity.

Our judgment of others constructs a bias wall between us and them. And while walls may somewhat protect or serve, they also isolate and restrict.

Here's What I Figure

I have interrupted God many times with my judgments, assessments, assumptions, and profiling. I've deduced that a particular event or person or thing is bad when all along I just didn't wait to see the completion of the whole picture. I seem to feel more in control when I can just slap a label on things.

THAT'S SOME NASTY FLOUR!

A restaurant owner walked into his kitchen while the chef was preparing a southern meal of chicken fried steak and mashed potatoes. While the chef had his back turned, the owner grabbed a spoon and helped himself to a big scoop of flour. "Pettewy! Yuck! That tastes terrible! You're a bad cook!"

The chef saw him spitting out the white cloud. "But wait! You haven't seen the whole picture. You're going to love the brown gravy I plan on whipping up with that flour!"

When you call something or someone "bad," it's like discounting the chef's culinary skills after tasting the white flour. And worst of all, you'll miss out on the chicken fried steak!

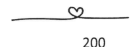

My most challenging moments as a parent were those choices made to reluctantly let go and allow my kids to live their own lives. Imagine that! Letting them make their own choices without my interference. I desperately wanted to protect them from what I saw as harmful or bad, but I also wanted them to benefit from their own bad choices.

When I'm quick to judge (and that's what we're doing with our good/bad labels), I'm not allowing life to unfold at its own natural pace.

Shakespeare wrote, "There is nothing either good or bad but thinking makes it so."

How often have you looked back on a job loss, or a break-up, or a missed opportunity, or an accident, only to think, "I'm so glad that turned out the way it did!" Heck, there's even a C&W song by Garth Brooks to remind us of this! "Thank God for unanswered prayers!"

My wife Franca has this one in the bag. Not long ago a road detour forced her off her schedule. She almost missed her appointment. And what did Franca do with that?

She thanked God for taking care of her. She told me, "There's no telling what I was protected from. What do you suppose might have happened if I had taken that original route?"

I think she's onto something. I think about all the mishaps from which I was unknowingly spared. Who knows what would have happened "if...?"

THE ATTITUDE OF GRATITUDE

Gratitude is a very empowering choice to make. Express thanks, even for those events or outcomes that may look bad in your eyes. "Thank you, Lord, for all those things that didn't happen. Thank you for working on my behalf. Thank you for seeing the big picture that is so invisible to my eyes."

Practice flipping your judgments. Hold back the verdict you want to assign to people and events and carry the attitude of gratitude. Then see what a difference it will make in the progression and outcome of your day. See how differently you'll engage with all of life around you.

1 Thessalonians 5:18 reminds us to give thanks for everything.

Everything!

My friend, you see only a portion of the truth in any given circumstance. You simply do not have enough information to bring down the gavel. And when you do so, you simultaneously erect self-imposed limits, detaching yourself from possible blessings, discoveries, connections, possibilities, valuable insights, lessons, and miracles.

BOTTOM LINE ⌣

I'm going to introduce you to the antidote to judgment. I want to sell you on a bottle of CURIOSITY! Guaranteed to keep you engaged and fascinated with life. Choose curiosity.

Your judging is usually based on partial and incomplete information. No matter how thin you slice it, there are always two sides.

Whatever you're looking for, you'll find it. If you look for the bad in folks, then by golly it'll show up clear as day. Whatever you focus on expands.

Climb outside of what you know in your brain because what you know is small compared to what you don't know. Get curious and stay curious! Starve your ego and feed your sense of fascination and wonderment. Ask more questions and make fewer statements.

Exercise the art of Empathy. Put yourself in their shoes and wonder what it must be like being them. This is not an exercise of "re-labeling," but rather of "un-labeling." I'm not asking you to agree with them, I'm wanting you to rid yourself of your own toxic premature assessments. I'm on your side. I want what's best for you!

Reminder

A great stress relief: Try less Judging & more Kindness

Your choice to label things and people does about as much good as your belly button. It serves no one. It just sits there and it's not even that pretty. As we say in the South, "It don't do squat." Even worse, it limits you, confines you, and closes doors.

Flip your choices. Practice choosing from love, empathy, and kindness. Catch yourself in the act of assuming. Shake it off, and then start actively looking for the good. Get curious. Your curiosity will find more goodness than you can shake a stick at.

SOME PEOPLE
FEEL THE RAIN,
OTHERS JUST
GET WET

Bob Marley

28

BLAME LESS,
OWN MORE

T̲H̲E̲ ̲S̲T̲O̲R̲Y̲ ̲W̲E̲ ̲T̲E̲L̲L̲ ̲O̲U̲R̲S̲E̲L̲V̲E̲S̲

It's not my fault. Well, most of it isn't my fault. I have to protect my pride. It's just not my fault.

FLIP IT   Whatever percentage of the blame you assign to others is the exact amount of growth you deny yourself.

"If at first you don't succeed, no worries!
Just blame your parents."
— Marcelene Cox

Blaming others for what happened or didn't happen, or for where you are or where you are not in life, gives you a momentary free pass. But there's a hefty price to pay for that pass.

Remember those old Tarzan episodes, where the bad guy seemed to always end up in quicksand? Those episodes kept me awake at night.

Emotional quicksand is the worst. Yep, even worse than the real stuff! It's called blame. It may not keep you awake at night, but it can sure keep you immobile and frozen in time. And eventually, like quicksand, it will swallow you up!

Your life probably fits into one of these two categories:

1. You are actively working toward your dreams and building the life you want.

2. You're blaming something or someone else for why you are not working toward your dreams.

I'm telling you this because I wish someone would have told me years ago. You may not feel like you're actually blaming but stay with me. You just might bust out of this chapter with a newly discovered secret superpower.

DON'T MAKE YOUR NEXT PAY FOR YOUR EX

Let's talk about that past relationship. You know, the one that started with love and infatuation, only to end in anger and disgust and a few verbal hand grenades? What did you do with that one? Where did you store it? Know it or not, you put it somewhere.

Did you store it in blame? "He threw me across the room and so I left." Or, "She changed on me, she emotionally abused me." Or, "He cheated on me." Regardless of what reason you used to pawn it off on "them," you missed it! You missed the gift.

Reminder

Blaming keeps your life on pause

I don't care how squeaky-clean you think you were in that relationship, there was something for you to learn about yourself. If you didn't get the lesson, then your next will pay for your ex.

Do not make your future friendships pay for your past bad ones. No matter how bad your past relationship was, find the value. Find the lesson. Or else you'll take the same unlearned lesson into the next one, and likely reap the same results.

What purpose did it play for you? What important insight about yourself did it try and deliver to you, that maybe you ignored because you were so busy trying to move on with your life? Don't give yourself a free pass by blaming others for your past failures.

WHAT'S YOUR REASON?

Picture in your mind, for a moment, the life you've always wanted. Maybe you've always wanted to live on an island or be a doctor. Maybe you've imagined starting a charity or owning a ranch. Now, give me one good reason why you're not pushing hard right now toward that dream. Come on, let's get honest. Which card are you playing? The lack of education card? Gotta raise those kids first? You're too young? You're too old? You're too much in debt? Not skilled enough? The timing isn't right? Or maybe whenever you get "a round tuit?" Too skinny? Too fat? Too hairy? Too gosh-darn handsome?

Whatever your one reason is, that's where you've mentally staked your blame. That's your convenient story you tell yourself because it serves you for the moment by keeping you sane, blameless, and guilt-free.

It serves you because, as long as you have something or someone to help you justify what you don't have, then it's really not your fault. After all, skinny people can't succeed doing that job, so why even try! And old people can't do that one either. (Tell that to Colonel Sanders, who started KFC at age sixty-nine.)

How convenient, not having to chase that dream or do the work required. You may even try convincing the world that you're completely satisfied. That was my position. I was outwardly happy and secretly unfulfilled. That was my story and I was sticking to it.

BEING VICTIM IS SO DARN COZY!

We victims don't have to take risks or face the rejections that come with dream-chasing. It's so much easier to just kick back and do what I have to do so I can pay the bills and keep my big screen TV. I'll adjust my pillow, check the thermostat, and make sure that there are enough eggs and milk in the fridge. Now, where in Sam Hill did I leave that TV remote?

Blame hides behind many disguises. But whatever disguise it wears, it still holds you hostage and is keeping you from fulfilling your life purpose. Look at all those masks! There's one called compassion. Then there's humility, bitterness, impatience, self-pity, innocent victim, and selflessness.

Here's What I Figure

We blame others to keep our sanity. It must be the economy's fault or the fact that these widgets I sell are out of style and the wrong color. Besides, that boss of mine is the one who's holding me back.

Something outside of myself is causing all this. I mean, it can't be me!

Remember the movie *City Slickers*? They talked about the "one thing" in life. When you get that one thing in place, then all the rest of life will come together for you. I believe we each have a common "one thing." We desire to feel OK about ourselves. We want to believe that we're not broken, that we're lovable and worth something. That unconscious need is gripping.

Reminder

Blaming is easy but owning it takes guts

Our blaming other people or things somehow helps us protect that feeling of OK-ness. But it's an endless effort of futility that keeps us tied to mediocrity.

Imagine your life having a remote controller with pause and play. Whenever you blame any lacking in your life on a person or thing, it's like handing them the remote control to your life. And their thumb is smack dab on your pause button! Blaming others is like putting your success on hold. This applies in your relationships, your money matters, and in your overall happiness.

 Blaming keeps you motionless, while you wait for things and people "out there" to change.

Here are a few ways we play the blame game:

🖑 "I'm in a marriage going nowhere because of him. I cannot do or say anything. I'm stuck."

🖑 "It's just too late in life for me to start another career."

🖑 "I have too much going on in my life to do that."

🖑 "I can't make money doing that."

🖑 "My partner isn't supportive."

🖑 "I'm not educated or skilled or smart enough."

🖑 "I would have to relocate, and I can't move right now."

🖑 "People will judge me if I did that."

🖑 "That's just not who I am."

These help to keep the sanity and self-esteem intact. You can borrow any of them you wish if you feel the need to stay stuck.

GOOD NEWS: YOU ARE NEVER REALLY STUCK

What do the words stuck, helpless, and victim have in common? They don't exist, except in your mind. You always have an out, an alternative choice. But you must choose it.

The most common excuse I've heard in troubled relationships is, "I have no choice. If I did that, the relationship would end!" Are you kidding me? Such a mind-set only keeps you on the fence while keeping your relationship plugged into a respirator. Truth must be present. You must be willing to let it set you free.

Any relationship will respond to the truth by either ending or growing, sinking or swimming. Down South, it's "either go potty or get off the darn pot!"

BOTTOM LINE

The first step to quitting the blame game starts with recognizing where it is that you are placing the blame. I'll give you some help: Make a statement right now, out loud, and say why you are not living out your dream. Right now, quickly. Whatever reason came to your mind is your chosen "free pass." That is your justification for not going full-out. And it certainly serves you, as you get a free pass from avoiding the risks and challenges that come with dream-chasing.

Some folks are physically impaired or have serious restrictions in life. I know things can seem impossible or unreachable at times. And I also know that many great people throughout history have reminded us that the human spirit can rise above any challenge thrown our direction.

Helen Keller, Nick Vujicic, Lily Rice, and Krystal Cantu are just a few stories that are worth reading about. Let them inspire you as you write your own story.

Own your part, claim your 100 percent capability to have everything your heart desires. Then work your plan. Refuse the temptation of the free pass. The next move is ALWAYS yours. So, what will be your next move?

Why don't we just mosey into the next chapter and talk about what's prompting you and me to blame?

29

FEEL THE FEAR AND
DO IT ANYWAY

THE STORY WE TELL OURSELVES

Me? Afraid? Naw. I'm just not cut out for that. Besides, it won't work anyway. Besides, I'm too busy, too fat, too young, or unqualified. Besides, this mediocre life isn't so bad.

FLIP IT Do you know what fear's kryptonite is? Movement. Get up and move toward your dream or your goal, and in the process fear will dissipate.

> *"Fear kills more dreams than*
> *failure ever will."*
> — *Suzy Kassem, poet*

Let's get real about this fear thing. We all have it. Maybe more than we want to admit. If you are not fully living the life you intended to live, fear is the culprit. Fear of failure, fear of success, fear of the unknown or the known, fear that you might fall in a hole or lose your money or get swallowed up by a man-size Gummy Bear. Fear that you won't be enough. Fear that you'll be worse off than you are now.

Fear can be grouped into one of two species: Biochemical or emotional. Your DNA carries a biochemical fear that's essential for your survival. Whenever you hear a noise in the front room or when your kitchen cup towel suddenly catches fire from the stovetop, your biochemical fear kicks in and you leap into all-hands-on-deck survival mode.

Without biochemical fear as part of our makeup, you and I would be jumping off cliffs and catching our hair on fire, just for the entertainment.

And then there's emotional fear that sabotages dreams and leaves its victim with remorse and regret. And if I can do my part in helping you avoid those regrets, then I'm all in. We can undo shoelaces, misspelled words, and light bulbs, but we can't undo regrets.

Fear is here, and it's real. And I'm convinced it's here for good reason. It actually performs a useful function, so let's flip that fear into something useful.

Fear is your reminder to pay attention, take caution and to be alert. Our problems start when fear becomes a stop sign. Let's redefine what fear is. It's a yield sign, not a stop sign.

Give yourself permission to be fearful, but not to use  it as an excuse to stop or retreat. Let it be a friendly nudge, alerting you to something that needs addressing, overcoming, learning, or healing.

If you don't own your fear, then your fear will own you. Grab it by the horns and say, "You're mine!" Now, this doesn't mean you won't feel the fear. This just means that you are the one calling the shots, not your fear.

Here's What I Figure

It's time to invite fear in for a cup of tea and a snack. No more ignoring or denying or hiding out from fear. Let's make peace with it. FDR was right: "The only thing we have to fear...is fear itself."

Fear will continue to debilitate your life until you FLIP IT. Flip what fear actually means to you, thereby flipping what you do with it. I got really good at ignoring fear. I was the best at it! I was a master diverter. But it kept rearing its ugly head for me to finally face it.

It helps me to stop and get straight on the facts. What's true and what's not true? When you break down and disassemble the thing that you fear, you'll soon realize that the thing you're fearing doesn't even exist! When you line up the facts, you'll always realize that fear isn't based in reality.

Reminder

Feed your Faith and your fear will starve

What you fear will or won't happen hasn't yet arrived. So, it's not real! That monster you fear is actually an extended shadow of a little mouse!

Let's consider my fear of failure. Yes, I'm afraid to fail. But wait, it doesn't exist, except in my mind. I have not yet failed. I fear rejection. But wait, rejection hasn't happened, so it's not real.

So much of what you fear simply isn't real. Oh sure, maybe it happened in your past. But let's get something straight: your past does not equal your present unless you deem it so. Gotta flip that thinkin'!

George Zalucki, author of *Straight Talk*, said, "My life was filled with terrible things! Some of which actually happened." Maybe you've seen the well-known acronym of fear: False Evidence Appearing Real.

The key to effectively removing any undermining force in your life is to choose its replacement, and then to observe a successful outcome from that choice.

So, what's driving your fear? The loss of money if you choose that investment? Rejection if you ask the question? Embarrassment if you choose to be vulnerable? Humiliation if you actually try and write that book? Failure if you take that leap?

What are you fearing in your life? This is the first critical step, a step often skipped, because we don't want to face that thing that we deep-down fear. We would rather just pour another glass of tea and talk about other less-threatening matters.

Here's what's at the root of our fears: We fear that we're simply not enough. And, by golly, we will do whatever it takes to avoid feeling not enough. We will jump through hoops or miss our favorite party just to avoid feeling unlovable, unacceptable, unsuccessful, unimportant, or unworthy.

Our biochemical fear runs from physical harm or death. Our emotional fear runs from the horrific notion that "I'm not OK."

Stand in front of a mirror and look at yourself. Really look. Standing in front of you is your best friend and, at the same time, your harshest critic. It's a dichotomy. Choose to feed one and starve the other.

Reminder

Flip that fear from a stop sign to a yield sign, then act on Faith ♡

The first one, your best friend, will take you to the moon and back. The second one will hold you back and suggest that you settle for mediocre.

Recognize, in every moment of your day, which of these two you are feeding. To which of them are you giving the inner microphone? Whichever one you give voice to wins.

Bottom Line ⌣

There's no way around this fear thing. You can't dance around it, dodge it, or pretend it's not there. You simply go through it. So, let's flip what you're making fear mean, and it will become much more palatable and penetrable, I assure you.

If you don't sacrifice for what you want, then the  things you want will become your sacrifice.

Stop overanalyzing. When push comes to shove, you simply have to feel the fear and do it anyway. Those who don't, lose. Those who do, win. Move your legs. Those are your best weapons.

I'll give you my Roberto's guarantee: When you feel the fear and then do it anyway, it will be like riding that roller coaster ride. You know, the one you refused to ride one hundred times earlier. When you finally get the nerve to ride it, and it finishes, you'll sigh and comment, "That wasn't nearly as bad as I thought it was going to be! Let's do it again!"

Faith is fear's antidote, and faith is an Action. Now go take Nike's advice and JUST DO IT.

30

FORGIVE AND
FREE YOURSELF

THE STORY WE TELL OURSELVES

Some things are unforgivable. Besides, they don't deserve my forgiveness. It's my right!

FLIP IT

Your choice to forgive is for you, not them. It sets you free. See it as Grace Paid Forward.

> *"Always forgive your enemies.*
> *Nothing annoys them so much."*
> — *Oscar Wilde*

Forgive. Not necessarily because they deserve it, but because you don't deserve to have to carry around the weight of your grudge.

The Shack, by William P. Young, does a masterful job of depicting one of the toughest acts of forgiveness. Mac brought himself to a painful place of choosing to forgive the man who murdered his daughter. This is an extreme case, but nonetheless has all the same moving parts of what you might face in forgiving your boss who lied, or your partner who deceived you, or your cousin who betrayed you, or your dog that just ate your favorite couch.

We actually have this forgiveness thing backward. Many see it as a gift to give someone else as if we're letting them off the hook. And to further the distortion, we think that we're punishing them by holding back our forgiveness.

It's a power-play. You feel betrayed, and now you have the retaliating upper hand. But nothing could be further from the truth. That belief will keep you handcuffed.

Forgiveness is not about the other guy deserving forgiveness; it's about you not deserving the toxic grudge that eats you from the inside-out.

Your ego can wear that poker face and refuse to acknowledge the damage from your grudge, but it's there. Aware of it or not, it's slowing you down.

 Withholding your forgiveness is like popping a poison pill in your mouth and expecting the other guy to die.

We've all been wronged. You may be carrying deep scars from being abandoned by your dad or being abused by a stranger or relative. Perhaps you're carrying crust that's so thick, you can't even remember where it started.

I was once burglarized while sleeping soundly in my own bedroom. Startled by a noise, I opened my eyes, only to be staring at the barrel end of a .38 special revolver. Then came the chilling scream I still remember: "On the floor, M.F.!" The gun against my nose convinced me to quickly obey.

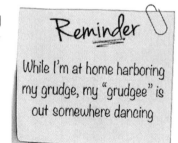

Reminder

While I'm at home harboring my grudge, my "grudgee" is out somewhere dancing

The next half-hour was out of a horror movie as I lay there tied up on my kitchen floor. It seemed like an eternity passed as I helplessly listened to the escalating rage of four angry men plowing through my stuff. I was certain that my life was about to end.

Obviously, I was spared. After a short period of silence, I looked up and they were all gone, along with my most prized possessions.

During the subsequent months, I carried with me a grudge. I deserved that grudge. It was mine, and they certainly didn't deserve my forgiveness.

I remember telling the story of that night to family and friends. And with each recounting, I felt my rage well up inside. It was my right to feel it, and, by golly, I exercised that right!

Reminder

To Forgive is a
Virtue of Strength

Did it serve me? Even though venting my rage felt good, my vindictiveness felt somewhat empty. There was no life, no value, no color in it. It had no end, no resolve, no movement. No nothing. I felt its empty nothingness.

Now, you may be thinking, "But I don't know how to forgive!" I'm with you. Some cases are tougher than others. And I'm not telling you it's easy. But I am telling you that it's necessary.

So, you were hurt? Let's take a look. This hurt that you're carrying around with you, as painful as it may be, is nothing more than a thought. It's just a thought!

And that thought of resentment, anger, or hatred is like a tourniquet around your joy. Your resentment will relentlessly continue to debilitate and disempower you.

YOUR GRUDGE IS YOUR KRYPTONITE

A worthy repeat: Your resentment is only a thought. Do not shackle your life to a thought. My house break-in was real at one moment in time, but it's no longer real. It's gone. It does not exist, except as a memory or thought. I now have a choice of what to make that memory mean.

I want you to know peace, true peace. And the entryway to peace is through forgiveness. You'll never know true peace with an unforgiving heart. Peace cannot coexist with that grudge, any more than oil with water, or my dog Roxie with the poor UPS man just trying to deliver a package.

HERE'S WHAT I FIGURE

In my experience, the hardest part of forgiving is taking that first step of surrendering the gavel. No! Don't take my gavel! It's my right! It's my power! It's my only way to get them back. And so, like a baby with his first binky, I have to somehow give it up. It takes falling on my bended knees, knowing that all is in safekeeping in God's hands. Forgiveness takes guts!

Giving up the judgment gavel is giving up my right that was never mine in the first place! It never was and never will be.

So, in essence, I'm releasing an imaginary possession, an illusion! I'm letting go of something I never owned. It never was and never will be my jurisdiction to hold judgment over another person.

Reminder

Forgiveness is the key that will unlock your own prison door

I'll say it again. Your grudge is just a thought, something you contrived in your mind. Sure, their words were real.

Their actions were real. Everything about the event was real. But it's not real anymore. It's gone. And you are left with its memory. And most importantly, you are left with what you are making that memory mean.

My friend, come sit right here and sip some of this fresh-ground dark-roast Colombian coffee with me. Let's look at this thing for what it really is. Clear your vision from past "ick" for just this moment and take a really deep breath.

Fix your mind on this: You and I were forgiven. That's why we have life; life through grace. Now, one of the most noble and high-road choices you will make in your lifetime is the choice to forgive. It's a choice of integrity that will give grace to your offender while giving love, peace, respect, and freedom back to yourself. This is truly one of life's win/win choices.

**My choice to forgive is simply my
receiving God's grace and paying it forward.**

My good friend Mattie shared a simple 3-step process that will help bring power and closure: Forgive, Release, then Bless. It's a powerful 1-2-3 punch that will set you free from the oppression of your own animosity.

I FORGIVE YOU. I give you the right to be who you are, and I acknowledge that I don't know what I don't know. You have your reasons and I have mine.

I don't have to like what you did, or even agree with what you did. I simply give you the grace to make your own moves and choices in life without my judgment or critique.

I RELEASE YOU. I choose to let go. I'm not in the business of keeping score and hoarding ill feelings like a packrat. I intend to soar in life, and to do so I must shed the weight of this impediment. So, I hereby cast off this burdensome resentment. Whooosh! Gone!

I BLESS YOU. This might be the most empowering and completing part of this process. I choose to go beyond letting go. I step beyond that and ask God to bless your life. I will not flick you away like a gnat, and then wash my hands of you. Instead, I choose to pray for your healing, renewal, and restoration.

For further help on this subject, I have attached an addendum at the back of this book. It's a powerful exercise by John Gray.

Wayne Dyer said, "Your life is like a play with several acts. Some of the characters who enter have short roles to play, others, much larger. Some are villains and others are good guys. But all of them are necessary, otherwise, they wouldn't be in the play."

Everything and everyone has their purpose in crossing your path, so open your senses and raise your radar. Look for the learning, and do not allow those barnacles called "grades and scores" to take root in your soul.

Bring to mind someone in your life whom you have not forgiven. It might be a small, insignificant grudge. But it's a judging spirit that keeps you from fully engaging with them. It could be someone who offended or betrayed or violated you. Or it could merely be someone you disrespect for their actions or words.

BOTTOM LINE

It's time to practice. C'mon, I'm not here just to look pretty. I'm here to walk you through this. Let's start with empathy. Blessings will surround you as you respond to people with empathy vs. judgment.

Empathy will literally help guard your heart against anger and upset. Proverbs 2:11 reminds us, "Discretion will watch over you, and understanding will guard you."

So practice the 3 above steps. Right now. Pick something simple. Start ridding yourself of the weight of resentment and judgment.

Not long after my house break-in, I took a mental journey. I traveled in their shoes as best as my imagination let me. I remembered they were uneducated and uncivil in their banter. So, it's a safe bet that they didn't have the cozy upbringing I was privileged with. And maybe they didn't benefit from having two parents in love.

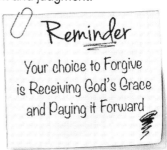

Reminder

Your choice to Forgive is Receiving God's Grace and Paying it Forward

I wondered what it was like being them. What was it like to grow up in a hostile and unsupportive environment?

My speculations helped me form an "empathy cover" over my animosity. And that empathy slowly began guarding my heart against my own harsh judgments.

I focused less on their guilt or innocence or ill-advised choices, and more on claiming my dignity and respecting them as human beings. I didn't agree with what they did, nor did I like it. Honestly, I hated it. I could not even begin to understand why anyone would pull off such a crime.

For me, the power of this exercise showed itself when I released them to my God and prayed for their souls in hopes that they will someday "get it." And I now pray that they will someday find this book. :o)

Don't allow your ego to cloud your vision of the freedom you'll enjoy when you rid yourself of that grudge.

To forgive is to receive God's grace, and then pay it forward. Choose freedom by choosing to forgive. It doesn't cost a dime, it has a sweet aftertaste, and it doesn't even add inches to your waistline. What a deal!

<I included for you an effective tool at the close of this book to help you through the process of forgiving. I hope it serves you>

PART FOUR

FLIP
YOUR DESTINY

31

EMBRACE
THE MYSTERY

THE STORY WE TELL OURSELVES

I'll be at peace when I figure things out. If I can understand why that happened and what will happen next, I'll then be at peace.

FLIP IT Embrace the mystery. When you don't have to have the answers and you can marvel at the things you don't understand, you'll then find peace that passes all understanding.

"The most beautiful thing we can experience
is the mysterious."
— Albert Einstein

Even the Brainiac of our era, Albert Einstein, understood the importance of letting go of the mind and relaxing in the spirit.

One year, on my birthday, my buddies blindfolded and kidnapped me. I had no idea what they were up to or where they were taking me.

After a ten-minute car ride, they led me into a room full of ruckus and people-noise. My friends made me stand up on a chair. As they helped me keep my balance, one of them removed my blindfold and, there I was! I looked around the room and realized I was on display at one of my favorite restaurants.

With everyone staring and laughing, the birthday song started off the celebration. Embarrassing? Yep. But I'll admit: it was tons of fun.

I could have fought and kicked and insisted on knowing what was going on. I could have bucked and insisted on knowing the itinerary, but that would have interrupted the entire process, while denying myself the experience of such a joyful ending.

Sometimes, I wrestle with why things happen, and why other things don't happen. Why was that mishap brought into my life? Why was he born like that? Why didn't I get that raise? Why do bad things happen? Why death? Why diseases? Why me?

I can drive myself batty, dwelling on questions to which I will never have the answer. That only keeps me bunched up while life passes me by.

How many times have you heard someone ask the question, "Why would a loving God allow that to happen?" Or "Why didn't God answer my prayers?"

This is where our minds work against us. We can't find the answer, so we often assume the worst. Some folks even deduce that there is no God, or that at least He must not be all-loving.

230

Our controlling nature insists on an answer, and when we can't find one, we make one up. That gives us a sense of feeling in control of matters. We just don't like not knowing the answers!

Here's What I Figure

We know so much, and yet we know so little. Science is able to put a man on the moon and manipulate DNA, but no one can figure out why deer always face north and south while grazing, or how it's possible for a field ant to carry five thousand times its own body weight. And can you believe that mighty oak came from a tiny seed? Holy cow!

I figure, my pea-brain can comprehend only so much. This world, and its natural order, is precise and downright ingenious! And so, I marvel.

Here's what I'm saying. There comes a time when it serves you to stop trying to figure out how the darn airplane can stay up in the air. Just accept that it does, otherwise, you'll miss the ride.

Bottom Line

Our need to feel in control robs us of those life-moments of appreciating and savoring the unexplainable.

Stop insisting on "knowing" or understanding things and people that you will never know or understand. That's only robbing you of the peace and joy of being in the present. Recognize when it's time to lay down the calculator and just go "wow!"

DO YOUR PARTNER & FRIENDS A FAVOR; FALL IN LOVE WITH YOURSELF

32

SELFISH PEOPLE
MAKE BETTER
LOVERS

THE STORY WE TELL OURSELVES

Life is about sacrificing for others, giving myself for the good of the whole. And to do so, I must deny myself. Selfless acts are noble acts.

FLIP IT The healthiest thing you can do for all of your relationships is to first love yourself.

*"Loving yourself isn't **vanity, it's sanity.**"*
— André Gide

Now, when I first heard this notion of self-love, I was taken back. Such an idea was a far cry from what my mama taught me since I was a rug rat. I can still hear her words, "Now, don't be selfish." I imagine we were all raised with similar advice.

Before any flight's takeoff, the attendant will give her or his speech to remind you that, in case of an emergency, you must place the oxygen mask on yourself first, before placing one on your child. Some of us know that spiel by heart, and it makes perfect sense. You're not worth much to your child if you can't breathe!

The oxygen mask is the story of life. If I don't carry my own oxygen supply, then I'll be fighting you for yours. Likewise, if I do not bring my own sense of self-love or self-worth into our relationship, then I will expect you to supply it for me. I'll need for you to make me feel better about myself. I will hold you against my expectations. Yikes! We've probably all experienced the receiving end of neediness, and it's not pretty.

HERE'S WHAT I FIGURE

Self-love is the key to effectively loving and serving others. The oxygen mask must go on yourself first. This is not selfish, this is self-loving. Taking care of yourself allows you to take care of others more effectively. Here's how self-love plays out in relationships:

When I'm OK with me, then I'm OK with you. The less "OK" I feel about myself, the more dependent I am on your compliments and affirmations and edifications. And I especially need for you to never suggest to me that, on some level, I'm not OK! A deal?

Reminder
Loving myself sets
me Free to
Love you

When you bring your own sense of worth and OK-ness into your relationship, you'll then be at peace with your partner and with exactly who they are. You will not feel the need to change them for your sake.

Your love for them will require nothing from them in return. You won't be disturbed by their flirtatious energy or their time spent away with friends. Your commitment to the relationship will be without conditions or agendas. And in that scenario love dances without strings.

Self-love looks like not needing your partner or friend to be anything that they are not! And this sets you free to love them for who they are, rather than for what they can do or be for you. This is huge!

LOVE FROM YOUR OVERFLOW

You must first have it to give it. You cannot give what you don't have. When your love for yourself overflows, you'll then have plenty to give to your partner or friend. When you are "good in your own skin," the love that you give will require no payback.

Here's the big trophy that comes with self-love. When you get right with yourself, when you become truly content with who you are, guess what happens then?  You'll no longer need others to provide your happiness or affirm your value or worth. Then you don't have to try so darn hard! You can just be you! Whoa! Did you get that?

But wait, it gets even juicier! When you don't need approval or support or validation from others, you can stop holding back. Yes! You can move past that tentative mind-set that keeps you weighing and assessing and wondering. You are free to just love them unconditionally! Ding ding ding! Ladies and gentlemen, may I present to you REAL LOVE.

"But wait a second. I want my partner to love me back! I do have some expectations of what I want them to be and do. What's wrong with that"?

Gosh, of course we all want support and approval from our partner and friends. I want to hear how handsome I look in my bow tie, or how super I am! I want to feel loved and appreciated. But there's a world of difference between what I *want* and what I *need*. "Want" desires love, but my "need" requires love. And, as we all know, neediness (expectations) is trouble brewin'.

SELFISH vs. SELF-LOVING

Here's the difference between selfish and self-loving: Selfishness assigns value to yourself, in relation to others. Self-love recognizes and honors your unique value to this world. The first is relative to others, while the second is relative to yourself. Self-love allows you to value others without a scorecard.

YOU HAVE IT ALL

You're really OK, just the way you are. You were made in God's image and let me just tell you: that's a mighty fine image! See, you really are all that and a bag o' chips.

There is a direct correlation between how much you love yourself, and how much others love you. Yep, when you truly love who you are, then you'll see others lining up behind you to love you as well. How 'bout them apples! Self-love attracts others, while selfishness repels.

Reminder

Self-care lets you give the world the Best of you, not the Rest of you

As odd as this concept may sound to some, I can assure you that this is key to your life firing on all cylinders. How you feel about yourself dictates every path you choose.

When I'm comfortable in my own skin, when I no longer have to fight for validation from you or from other people and things, I then no longer need my world around me to reinforce my sense of value.

I no longer have to have that fast car, big house, words of adoration, awards, or even success! No siree, Bob. These things are certainly great to have, and I love having them, but they are much sweeter when they're not the source of my happiness, but rather, an offspring of my happiness.

If you are a self-loving salesman, you can confidently ask for the sale, because you know that the rejection isn't about you or your value to this world. In starting your business, you'll not hesitate to reach for the stars, because failure isn't as fearful. You'll understand that it's not a reflection of your value or worth. In your relationships, you can tell the truth without worry of losing your friend or partner, because your happiness is not contingent on them staying. You are literally set free to just be you.

CRITICAL OF OTHERS?

If you find yourself critical of others, I have your answer: YOU. That's it. Now, this may be a hard pill to swallow, but here's the loving truth you can put in that pipe of yours and smoke:

The more you accept yourself, the more accepting you will naturally be with everyone around you.

Conversely, any disdain or rejection of others is a reflection of your own self-disdain. Your critical spirit says more about you than it does about them. This is useful info, as life again shows you what parts of that squeaky wheel need the grease.

 Taking care of you first results in your competent ability to take care of others around you.

I was a single parent raising Jess and Alex after their mother passed away. I used to love Country & Western dancing. I still do. I believe the C&W dance floor is the last frontier where one can hoot and holler in public without being arrested.

I made a choice back then that served all of us. I chose to not stop doing what I loved after their mother passed away. And that included dancing. So, on occasion, I gave my children their own play night while I enjoyed an evening of dancing. Choosing to take care of myself absolutely equipped me to be a better, stronger, and happier dad for my kids. They can attest to it.

On the other hand, I have known single moms who don't allow themselves the luxury of playtime. They see themselves as the sacrificial martyr, denying themselves for the sake of their kids. As noble as their intentions are, they consequently present themselves to their children torn and worn out.

BOTTOM LINE ⌣⌣

Let's shift how you hold this thing called self-love. Picture yourself, for a moment, the sole provider and guardian of a five-year-old. How will you take care of that child? You'll feed her the right foods. You'll make sure she chooses healthy friends. You'll clothe her and edify her with your words. You'll do everything you can to give her a healthy, balanced life.

YOU...are that child. I want you to take care of yourself, as you would for that five-year-old. Treat yourself to everything mentioned above. Be a good steward of your role as guardian of yourself, because that's what you are. Make the good and healthy choices, and in doing so, your world around you will change for the better in every aspect.

Not only will others treat you with the same level of respect you treat yourself, you'll be much more tolerant and accepting of those in your life.

Reminder

The more OK I am with me, the more OK I will be with you and with everything you say and do

It's a win/win deal, so FLIP IT! Flip the way you see selfishness vs. self-loving. Get clear on your value as a person. Know that you are made by a loving Maker, in His own image. The more value and worth you see in yourself, the more value you'll see in others. You'll make healthier choices for yourself, while your acceptance of others will bring you new acquaintances and possibilities.

33

ARE YOU A
VESSEL OR A CLOG?

THE STORY WE TELL OURSELVES

I'm the self-appointed sheriff in this domain. It's my job to make some things happen, and to stop other things from happening. Take that bull by the horns! If it is to be, it's up to me!

FLIP IT Life flows when you join the flow, not when you try and create the flow. You're either the vessel or the clog.

> *"Some folks make things happen, other folks watch things happen...and still others wonder, what the heck just happened?"*
> — Anonymous

You're either flowing with life, or you're trying to make life flow with you.

Are you helping or hindering the flow? You're either allowing or your resisting. There's no middle ground, because even in that middle-of-the-road passivity, you're a big clog.

Let's do a little "imagination painting." What would your disposition look like if you could paint a picture of it? Does it look noisy or calm? Would there be mismatches and chaos, or would there be colors flowing into other colors with grace and ease? What do your innards look like?

HERE'S WHAT I FIGURE

I grew up playing sports. I never really enjoyed watching; I wanted to play the game! I'm learning that there's a time to play the game, as well as a time to watch the game. There's a time to be on the court and taking charge, and there's an equally important time to be in the stands observing, learning, and cheering.

One of the most exciting lessons of "growing up" is realizing that life doesn't need me to hold its hand through everything. It can actually function on its own. Imagine that!

When I'm the vessel, I allow things to happen, rather than trying to make them happen. In doing so, I set the stage for those unexplained happenstances we call miracles. God, in His usual gentlemanly fashion, doesn't force His way in. His love is timeless and patient. When I get in the way, He seems to always give me another chance around the next corner. For that I'm humbly grateful.

WAYS WE CLOG THINGS UP

In conversations, you may be rushing dialogue, rather than listening. You may be offering up more statements than questions. You may be avoiding uncomfortable topics. You may not be expressing your truth.

With daily life, you may be staying so busy that the noise of your life is drowning out life's messages and God's voice. Your actions may be keeping you from hearing your own inner voice. You may be gripping your plans so tightly that things cannot happen on their own. Your fear may be keeping you bunched and stagnant.

With love, you may be "trying" rather than allowing. Love is an energy you can never contain. You can only be it, enjoy it, and give it. Anything beyond that, you're clogging it! Remember, love has no scorekeeper, no judge, and no ownership.

With relationships, maybe you are trying to "own" their stuff while protecting them from pain, discomfort, and challenges. And in doing so, you're isolating them from their own growth. Your attempts to help them could very well be hurting them. Be the vessel, allow your friends to have their stuff, while not pushing your stuff off onto them.

With finances, money is an energy. It's here for you to channel, not hoard. Flip your poverty mind-set and know that money is limitless. The more you give, the more you'll understand this spiritual truth. Be the vessel, even with your funds. Contribute, help, let go and tithe. You will make way for more money to flow to you and through you.

In your spiritual walk, you may be smothered by "religion" that's keeping you from "relation" with God. Rituals and repetition can have you "going through the motions," potentially clogging your eyes and ears and senses from discernment and true connection with your Maker. Don't allow your traditions to keep you from intimacy with God.

IN MY GARDEN

I like growing tomatoes and potatoes in my summer garden. Whenever I see the first sprout popping through the soil, I do what I can to nurture it. I don't try rushing it, forcing it, or manipulating it in any way. I create its environment to be as rich and nurturing as possible.

That's life. That's marriage, that's love, that's parenting, that's business. You and I are here to support its natural path.

With my garden, I am a student of what brings me the best crop. I study fertilizers and alkaline balances. The same holds true for life. Become a student of love and life itself. Learn what feeds love, and what starves love. Be an observer not an obstructer.

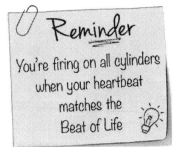

Be about the business of providing what people around you need in their lives. Provide what surroundings they need, whether it be encouragement or space. And then sit back and watch life unfold right before your eyes.

You have to learn the dance. You have to know what's your business and what's God's business. It's not difficult to see the difference. Your stuff is all about giving, not taking. It's all about contribution. It's all about gratitude for what you have. Your part is working hard and laying the supporting groundwork. God's business is in directing and clearing your pathway.

The serenity prayer says it well:
God grant me the serenity to accept the things I cannot change, Courage to change the things I can, And wisdom to know the difference.

I want you to enjoy Power in your life. I want you to witness miracles that move and propel and heal and mend and explode with celebration! My desire for you is that you see life as what it is, a plethora of opportunities where peace and love and joy and possibilities for success are boundless.

BOTTOM LINE

FLIP IT! No longer view your life as a chessboard of people and things available for your maneuvering and delegating and manipulating. Oh sure, you have to tell your kids what time to go to bed and tell your employees what their assignments are. But beyond that, back off! Do your part, set the stage, then allow people and things the chance to unfold at their own pace and timeframe. Allow others to make their own good and bad decision.

Be a facilitator, not an inhibitor. Be a seed, not a rooting warthog. Know when it's time to observe. Be that vessel that allows God to do His work. Be the landscape that allows life to flow where it intends to flow.

Know that there is a purpose and a masterplan that doesn't require implementation by you. Things may not turn out the way you pictured, or even insisted they would. Thank God they don't always! The more you let go and be the vessel, the more in awe you'll become, as life reminds you of what's truly best for you.

34

HIT REFRESH ON
YOUR BELIEFS

THE STORY WE TELL OURSELVES

I don't even know what I believe. But it doesn't matter. I'll just keep living the dream, doing the best I can.

FLIP IT You have a set of beliefs you bought into long ago. And your life circumstances are proof of those beliefs. Let's align your beliefs with what you want in life.

"If you think you can, or you think you can't...You're right."
— Henry Ford

Your life circumstances are a mere reflection of your inner beliefs.

I loved growing up in the era chosen for me. Those were simple times of board games and BB guns. The word "text" meant something entirely different. And the phone was...OK, you are not gonna believe what I'm about to say, so hold on to your saddle...Your phone was for making phone calls!

TV screens were smaller, and the remote control was whosever turn it was to get up and go turn the channel knob. I was the youngest in the family, and somehow it seemed like it was always my turn. Sunday evenings were typically family TV nights, and my favorites were *Bonanza* and anything that starred Roy Rogers.

I paid attention when Roy jumped off his horse Trigger and wrapped the reins around the hitchin' post with one whipping motion. I was bewildered how that itty-bitty strap always held that big horse to that post. Why didn't Trigger just walk away? He was so much bigger than that dinky strap!

Even more mesmerizing was when the circus came to town. Those huge elephants were kept by a little rope. A rope! C'mon, an elephant? A 12,000-pound elephant, being held back by a little rope? Are you kidding me?

That elephant was me! Yep, I'm an elephant, and my restricting beliefs are my little ropes. And I'll bet you have ropes too.

This was an empowering "Ah-ha" for me, and I hope it will be for you as well. That rope was big in the eyes of the baby elephant. But as that elephant grew older and bigger, it never occurred to him that he outgrew the rope. Nobody told him. And so, just like us, he lives out his life limited by his old beliefs.

You and I are literally living life based on some beliefs that were invented by a five-year-old!

Here's What I Figure

Toads don't really give you warts, and if you eat a mess of watermelon seeds, thankfully a watermelon tree won't really grow inside your tummy. As kids, we bought into ideas that aren't true. And the most damaging ones were the ones you bought into about yourself.

 There's an invisible world that rules your life. It's the world of your inner beliefs.

I want you to identify the limiting "ropes" in your life. What message did you receive and buy into as a child that you've unconsciously carried into your adult years?

☜ "I'm a social nerd. An outsider."

☜ "I'm too fat or too skinny, and therefore ugly or undesirable."

☜ "I'm worthless, because my parent told me I am."

☜ "I'm stupid, because I didn't get my degree."

☜ "I'm born into a poor family, and that's just what I'll stay."

☜ "I'm unlovable."

☜ "I have no real purpose."

☜ "I'm not talented like the others."

What is your small, unconscious belief about yourself that keeps you tied to the post?

My friend, know that you are bigger than that rope. You outgrew those beliefs that you claim are holding you back. They cannot contain you, except your believing they can. God's got this. He even stamped "fearless and enough" on your forehead when you came outta the oven.

Reminder

Beliefs win out over Efforts every time. Make certain your Beliefs are not opposing your Efforts

We each painted our own Picasso when we were young. We formed an image in our mind of what life is like and what it all means. Many of us are still living by those meanings.

Wake up! Awaken to what limiting beliefs you've been unknowingly carrying through these years. Those beliefs are only childhood lies that you outgrew long ago. It's time to shake them off! So much more life is waiting for you, beyond the reach of those confining, restricting ropes! But you'll never know until you take the bull by the horns and decide to break through those limiting beliefs.

I believed I'm not a writer. Well guess what...I'm a writer! I decided it's time to stop allowing my old beliefs to dictate my path. Yeehaw!

BOTTOM LINE 〜

A common question I'm asked is, *"How do I change my belief?"*

A belief changes when you introduce yourself to new conflicting evidence. And with repetitive interaction with that new evidence, your old belief eventually dissipates.

- I believed he was conceited, until I spent time with him and recognized that he was simply shy. New evidence changed my old belief.

- Horses scared me after I was bucked off once. I chose to get back up there and ride again. After a dozen times (new evidence), my new experiences changed my belief.

- Water was frightening until I learned to swim. My new experiences, over time, changed my belief about water.

- Relationships were hard, until I learned and practiced and grew. My new experiences shifted my old belief.

You can "mantra" all day long about a new belief. But until you put it into action and see new results, you'll still be significantly ruled by that old belief.

THE CHILDHOOD TRUTH

Here's the scoop about those messages you heard as a child: Many of the messages you thought you heard, you never really heard! Your "I'm unlovable" message from your dad was about his busy schedule, not about your lovability. The "You're stupid" message you heard from that kid on the playground was all about that kid, not about you. And that complex you formed because you didn't make the football team? It had nothing to do with your worth!

It serves you to remember that what others say about you says more about them than it does about you.

You're an adult now. It's time to anchor new beliefs. It's time to start redefining what things mean. It's time to wake up! Awaken to what unconscious beliefs are keeping you roped to life's hitchin' post.

You outgrew your tennis shoes and you certainly outgrew your beliefs. So choose and practice new ones. Flip your old beliefs into new, empowering beliefs. Act on that new belief and see new results begin to transform your life.

Change your base beliefs and change your very destiny!

35

YOU'RE OK!
NO, REALLY...
YOU ARE!

THE STORY WE TELL OURSELVES

It's not proper to think I'm awesome, or to think of myself as special. That's just downright egotistical. Isn't it?

FLIP IT You are always trying to prove to yourself and the world that you are "OK." Funny thing is, you already ARE OK.

"I'm OK cuz God don't make junk!"
— Anonymous

A wise man lay on his death bed, feeling content and fulfilled from his long life-journey. All was right with his soul. He sensed someone in the room. He glanced to his side and saw one of his great-grandchildren staring. The child asked, "Papa, what's the one most important thing I should know about life?"

The old man paused and thought for a moment, as if to sum up all the years into one lesson. With a gleam in his eye he turned and softly whispered, "Learn to love who you are and all of life will fall into place."

We touched on this in the previous chapter, and it deserves a roaring curtain call.

THE MAP

A dad was sitting in his favorite recliner one Saturday morning. He rarely had time for himself, and so he seized the moment with his newspaper and his coffee. Suddenly, his precious window was interrupted. His five-year-old son came running in. "Daddy, can we play?" As much as he loved his son, he didn't want to lose this rare moment of solitude.

Then, ping! He had a genius idea. He looked over at his son and said, "Tell you what, I'll come play with you after you piece this puzzle together."

> **Reminder**
> When everything
> around you is not OK,
> remember...
> You're still OK! :)

The dad then tore out a full-page map of the world from a back page. He ripped the entire page into many small pieces. "Now, take this paper puzzle of a map into the playroom. And after you've taped all the pieces together correctly, we will play."

Off dashed the eager boy. Relieved, the dad settled back into his easy chair with an exhale. He knew that he had easily bought himself two more hours of peace and solitude.

Only fifteen short minutes passed before the son enthusiastically dashed back into the room, shouting, "Done! Here ya go, Pop. Now can we play"?

The dad was stunned! This just wasn't possible! He looked down at the boy and asked, "How did you tape the world map together so fast, son?" The boy answered, "Easy. On the other side is a picture of a man. I just pieced the man together, and when I flipped it over, the world was complete."

As you pull yourself together, the world around you pulls together as it makes more sense and falls into place. You've been treating the world like a chess set, moving people and things and events and purchases around like chess pieces, trying hard to keep them all on track. But no one seems to cooperate!

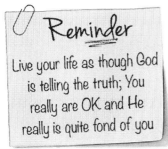

Reminder

Live your life as though God is telling the truth; You really are OK and He really is quite fond of you

We each have a deep-seated need to be "OK" with ourselves. We want to believe that we fit in, that we're accepted and lovable, that we're not defective, and that we make a difference. You've geared much of your life around both proving that you're OK while avoiding any suggestion that you're not OK.

You avoid embarrassment (that'll show you're not OK). You show your best side (to project that you're OK). You defend yourself when you're late, wrong, or foolish (you don't want to appear not OK). You want to have nice things (that'll show that you're OK). You avoid risks to evade failure (failure means you're not OK). You dress nice and act socially acceptable, so others will see you as OK.

It's all about feeling OK with ourselves. We must show our world that we're not broken or defective or worse, that we're not worth loving. Yikes!

My friend, this is powerful stuff! There exists an unconscious drive within us to prove that we're OK. And that dictates what you and I do and say, and how we think and feel.

So, what would life be like if you had no dog in that fight? What if you were truly, truly OK with who you are? What if you were not motivated by what you fear people think about you? What if your energy could be put into better campaigns, such as building a successful business or marriage or parent relations with your children? What if you didn't have this invisible ego-based pressure to prove to yourself and the world that you are OK?

HERE'S WHAT I FIGURE

Sit right here with me. I do want you to experience the freedom of truly being OK and at peace with everyone and everything in your life. I'm not talking about never having issues with things or people. I'm talking about the ability to make peace with everything, regardless of how irritating or disruptive it may be.

 You are priceless in God's eyes. Now stay with me; I'm not giving a sermon here. This is power-filled stuff. When you truly grasp just how fond your Maker is of you, you'll begin to experience unconditional self-love.

I'm not referring to church or religion. I'm talking about God, your Maker. Be careful not to allow those past religious filters to distort this pivotal message I have for you.

Loving yourself has nothing to do with perfection or talent or looks or acts. It has everything to do with knowing who you are. And knowing who you are is knowing who made you.

When you truly get that, when you truly receive God's pure love for you, then your sense of value will run deep like a river.

So, go forward and serve others, but never at the expense of honoring yourself. You must have an endless fuel supply to give fuel to others. Know that you are OK. You are made for love, by love.

BOTTOM LINE 〜〜

Max Lucado reminds us to LIVE LOVED. Live life as though you know that God loves you, because He does. And live as though He's quite fond of you, because He is. This is a powerful insight. When you get it, really get it, you'll begin recognizing the value and worth you bring to this world.

Now, take that new deep-seated belief into all your relationships and dealings. It will dramatically transform them all as you begin attracting and experiencing love and respect on levels you never knew were possible.

Reminder

"Live Loved"

—Max Lucado

THE PURPOSE
OF LIFE IS A
LIFE ON
PURPOSE

36

LIVE YOUR LIFE
ON PURPOSE

"Life: it's an unfolding string of opportunities delivered directly to you for your benefit."
— Rob

You've made it! You've arrived at my final chapter. It's time to bring it all together. My prayer is that you have gained one insight that helps you flip your thinking and live your life more "on purpose."

Your entire life has been like a play. Everything and everyone crossing your path has been cast into their unique and vital role to help further your journey. No happenstances, no coincidences, no accidents.

Many of us tend to "numb out" when we face discomfort, pain, or confrontation. While our defense mechanisms may keep us from having to face adversity, they also shield us from life itself.

I'm convinced adulthood is one big wake-up call.

GOOD MORNING LIFE, I'VE MISSED YOU!

I encourage you to start living your life more "on purpose." Grab life and gobble it up like a southern pecan pie! From your parenting to your partnering, from your career to your friendships, the whole shootin' match is waiting for you to wake up and smell the pan-roasted coffee.

WAKE UP, YOU PARENTS!

Start parenting your kids more on purpose. They are learning from your every inflection, emotion, and expression. Share with them the gems from this book.

Life tends to nudge us all toward following the herd. Yikes! Save your kids from the herd! Help them discover meaning and purpose. Actively support them on the path to their own purpose and reason why they are here. Warning: Their purpose may not look like your own purpose, and it just may not look like the purpose you have planned for them. So, brace yourself for the lesson of letting go!

Reminder
The Purpose
of Life is a
Life on Purpose

WAKE UP YOU LOVEBIRDS!

Remember, it's not about catching and keeping love in your life. It's far beyond that. Begin seeing your partner not only as a gift, but as your helpmate and even as your teacher. Commit to learning with them, as well as from them. Adopt a mission together; make a difference in this world. Then watch your love become a solid rock. Be their helpmate as you cheer them on toward living out their own purpose.

Patience, acceptance, and respect are all part of your homework assignment as you pro-actively practice love. Don't settle for less; love on purpose.

WAKE UP YOUR FRIENDSHIPS!

Have the guts to create your friendships more "on purpose." Learn the song in your friend's heart and sing it back to them when they forget the words. No more passive support from you. Assertively help them navigate toward their own passions and dreams. Remind them of who they are and of what they want from this life. Now we're talking friendship on purpose!

When you live your life on purpose, you'll begin recognizing how everything and everyone in your path is here for a reason. Each and every circumstance, good or bad, is presenting itself to you by no accident. Nothing is arbitrary. Everything has for you an intentional gift.

WAKE UP YOUR CAREER!

What is life about if not for contribution to others. That's why it lifts your spirits when you bake cookies for your neighbor, or you give that ten-dollar bill to that homeless guy. Now, you may be thinking, "How can I do my job or career on purpose?" Easy! Contribute! Let your job or business make a difference in the great scheme of things. Otherwise, you're just treading water.

Zig Ziglar said, "You can have everything in life you want, if you just help other people get what they want." For you realtors, stop trying to make money and start helping others find their dream home. You pencil-pushers, stop going through the motions for the paycheck and discover the good in what you are doing for others. You entrepreneurs and waiters and forklift operators, grab ahold of your WHY and let that WHY be about serving and contributing. Then watch your career take a giant leap forward.

MAKE YOURSELF UNSTOPPABLE

Once you have recognized that everything around you is here for your benefit, you'll power your way through challenges and roadblocks. Nothing and no one will be able to hold you back from extraordinary performance! Everything and everyone will take on new meaning, which will change your interactions with them. In turn, those shifts will attract new results.

Not only is everyone and everything playing an important role in your life-play, you are also playing an important role in theirs.

WHAT DOES LIVING ON PURPOSE LOOKS LIKE?

What was that? You never noticed that before now! Every minute becomes an adventure as you begin seeing things you didn't see before. It becomes evident that everything is here, not to just feed and entertain you, but to advance and promote you.

You'll become more aware of who you are as your choices align more with the things you most love and value.

You will begin noticing God's metaphors and messages that have been there all along. You'll catch yourself acknowledging and appreciating things you never paid much attention to before. Sunsets have never looked so spectacular! You'll perceive God's nudges, reminders, and His messages everywhere.

When you begin living more on purpose, it's like stepping off the repetitive, predictable merry-go-round and choosing the roller coaster. You'll experience the dips and turns and ups and downs and thrilling jerks of acceleration. You'll feel more alive than ever as you sense every bump and turn life throws at you. It's a bit scarier than the safety of that old merry-go-round. But somehow you know that at the end of the ride, you'll be just fine.

There's no longer need to avoid, run from, or ignore challenges. They're all a part of the plan that's for your own good.

And when you're out of tune with life, you'll remember that it's only a sour note sounding from your own fears. And you'll smile, reminding yourself to simply fall back into faith.

You will feel the freedom of letting go. No need to toil or grind or push against people or events as you find favor with the lessons on your plate.

You will expect less from others as you encourage them toward their own purpose rather than toward yours.

 Living your life on purpose will allow you to experience the joy of receiving, as well as giving.

Religion will take on a whole new meaning. It's no longer a structure where you tried housing God (as if He could ever be housed). God will become less "religion" and more "relation."

You will experience the ultimate life high as you receive God's loving embrace. Sure, you will face the same duties and tasks. You'll still have bills to pay, chores to do, and mouths to feed. But your new perspective reframes them all. They mean something different to you now.

Reminder

Stop letting life happen to you and start Creating your life on Purpose

Living life on purpose lifts you from the bleacher seats to the playing field, from the audience to the stage. Life becomes more real than you ever imagined as all your senses burst into full color! Even death makes sense to you now, as it no longer represents the last chapter in this eternal celebration.

And somehow, you're OK with not having all the answers. You feel peace from your faith rather than from your false sense of control.

Whatever path your journey takes you on, my friend, my prayer is that you see the messages all around you. Life and all its props and characters are here for your benefit. And they've all be pointing you back toward home. Back to you, back to your source, back to God. Living life on Purpose invites you to BE STILL AND KNOW THAT HE IS GOD, and all will be well with your soul.

This tool can help you work through the process of forgiveness...

GOOD-BYE/COMPLETION LETTER
(FROM *WHAT YOU FEEL YOU CAN HEAL* BY JOHN GRAY, PH.D)

DEAR_____

I'm writing you this letter to acknowledge, embrace, and release my feelings, and to discover and express the love and forgiveness that you deserve as a human being.

Level 1: ANGER
I don't like…
I resent…
I feel frustrated…
I want…

Level 2: SADNESS
It hurts…
I feel disappointed…
I feel sad…
I feel unhappy…
I wish…

Level 3: FEAR
It is painful…
I feel worried…
I feel afraid…
I feel scared…
I need…

Level 4: REMORSE & APOLOGIES
I apologize…
I feel embarrassed…
I am sorry…
I feel ashamed…
I am willing…

Level 5: LOVE, UNDERSTANDING, GRATITUDE AND FORGIVENESS
I love…
I appreciate…
I realize…
I forgive…
Thank you…
I would like…
I trust…
Goodbye.

263

FURTHER
ACKNOWLEDGMENTS

Every author has her or his "mountain" where the noise of the world can be left behind to work on the current project. My mountain was Las Brisas Farm in the Texas Hill Country.

Kathy and Eldon Aydelotte, you folks always provided a cozy, serene getaway that helped make this book a reality. You understood my mission and respected my passion. You were instrumental in helping me fulfill my vision for this book, from conception to publication.

It takes folks like you to inspire and create great things. Love to you both.

ABOUT THE AUTHOR

This is where the author typically dazzles you with his or her credentials, trophies and accolades. Surprise! No dazzle for sale here.

I'm Rob, and I'm as downhome as they come. Somewhere along my path I discovered something others were starving for; a way to put life in perspective where it all makes perfect sense. Where pain is gain and setbacks are necessary. Where making your move requires being still and vulnerability is your power.

I've been told more than a few times that my unconventional perspective coupled with my non-schooling serves me and others. I agree. I certainly have no interest in impressing you with knowledge or inundating you with solutions. I want to be effective with you. I want to make a difference in your life. I want your time with me to pay you back 100-fold.

No doubt I see things outside the box of conventional teaching (thank God!). During those college monologues I fought like a cat in a pool to distance myself from what I saw as cramping definitions and analyses.

I grew up in Houston, Texas, raised by Bob and Polly Cross (my two favorite folks). They were high school sweethearts and romanced their way through nearly 50 years of marriage before Dad passed on. He was my best friend. I counted it a privilege to have had a front row seat to watch real love in action.

Then...it was my turn. And I failed. Yep, I failed at marriage and I failed in business. Ouch! Yet, true to life, those turned out to be the greatest teachers of all! They were far more effective and more useful than any college class.

While others asked the "why" questions, I've always asked, "why not?" Through my bad decisions, mishaps and challenges I eventually learned to own my part in every piece of my past. Wow, what power I discovered! And I soon began helping others discover the same.

My dedication to growing beyond the limits of conventional education eventually led me to the love of my life, Franca. She and I have had a ball building our home in Sugar Land, Texas, while putting it all into practice.

I believe God made you and me with specific gifts and talents, factory installed. As for me? I'm a whittler and inviter. God blessed me with the passion and the ability to take life's everyday situations and whittle them down to the simple, basic, practical truths. And then I invite you to join me.

 Bottom line, my credentials are in the lives I have touched and help strengthen through the years. My trophies are my children. I believe the health and vitality of one's kiddos can shout volumes about the parent. Proof's in the puddin', baby!

About that guy; you know, the selfish one parked in front of me in the right lane at the world's longest red light? That jaybird has no intentions of turning right and it just burns my toast. And I feel distraught when my favorite baseball team loses. I have a fetish for pecan pie and frozen margaritas, and I may or may not get water in my eyes watching Hallmark movies (I'll deny that one if you share it).

I love my heavenly Father with all my heart. And even if I don't know your name, I love you and desire your best. And that is my strongest passion, to tell you the good news, in my distinctive language, and hope my words somehow make a profound difference in your life.

In short, I am gifted, purposefully called, zealously in love with life itself, and I am humbled to be here and to share it all with you.

Please feel the freedom to contact me at any time. I'm not just here to look perdy, you know; I want to help further your journey however I can. Come see me at RobFlips.com. Oh, and don't forget your free gift at RobFlips.com/special2021

From love and with a mountaintop anticipation for you!

Thank you Zandra
Thank you Leah
Thank you Lance
Thank you CeeCee
Thank you Susie
Thank you Franca
What a team! You were each instrumental in helping polish and present this book, all to make a difference in this world.